Praying for America

40 Inspiring Stories *and* Prayers *for* Our Nation

Dr. Robert Jeffress

Faith Words

New York • Nashville

FaithWords
Hachette Book Group
1290 Avenue of the Americas, New York, NY 10104
faithwords.com
twitter.com/faithwords

First Edition: June 2020

FaithWords is a division of Hachette Book Group, Inc.

The FaithWords name and logo are trademarks of Hachette Book Group, Inc.

The publisher is not responsible for websites (or their content) that are not owned by the publisher.

The Hachette Speakers Bureau provides a wide range of authors for speaking events. To find out more, go to www.hachettespeakersbureau.com or call (866) 376-6591.

Library of Congress Cataloging-in-Publication Data has been applied for.

ISBNs: 978-1-5460-1792-9 (hardcover); 978-1-5460-1793-6 (ebook)

Printed in the United States of America

LSC-C

10 9 8 7 6 5 4 3 2

To Scott Baker, Ed Yates, Sherry Forester,
and my nearly five hundred Pastor's Prayer Partners
at First Baptist Church, Dallas.

Thank you for faithfully praying for me, our church,
our nation, and our world as we share
the good news of Jesus Christ before His return.

Contents

★ ★ ★

INTRODUCTION

★ ★ ★

America's Only Hope

E *Pluribus Unum*—"Out of many, one."
This is the traditional motto of the United States of America.
From the first shots of the American Revolution to the British
surrender at Yorktown when we won our independence, thirteen
diverse colonies fought as one. And though passions threatened our
unity during the process of ratification, in the end, compromise
and conviction led to a Constitution that has become the envy of
the world.

However, since *E Pluribus Unum* first appeared on the Great
Seal of the United States, Americans, with the exception of the time
during the Civil War, have never been more divided. Today, our
nation seems to be closer to *Unum De Multis*—"Out of one, many."

How did we get to this state of division? We could blame the
radicalization of our universities, the degradation of our culture, or
the politicization of our everyday lives. We could blame America's
disunity on the breakdown of the family, the incivility we see in the
news and on social media, or the church's loss of cultural influence.
But it all comes down to a simple answer: We have forgotten God.

When people no longer love God, they can no longer love
themselves rightly. The equation is simple: When we cease loving

God, we cease loving ourselves; when we cease loving ourselves, we cease loving our neighbors. Psalm 9:17 warns that "the nations who forget God" will perish. But before they do, they will lose their unity and freedom.

On March 30, 1863, after the terrible loss of life at Antietam and the disaster of Fredericksburg during the Civil War, President Abraham Lincoln issued a proclamation appointing a national day of fasting and prayer. Recognizing that nations, as well as individuals, "are subjected to punishments and chastisements in this world," the president wondered whether "the awful calamity of civil war…may be but a punishment, inflicted upon us, for our presumptuous sins."

What did Lincoln identify as the nation's sin at that time?

We have forgotten God. We have forgotten the gracious hand which preserved us in peace, and multiplied and enriched and strengthened us; and we have vainly imagined, in the deceitfulness of our hearts, that all these blessings were produced by some superior wisdom and virtue of our own. Intoxicated with unbroken success, we have become too self-sufficient to feel the necessity of redeeming and preserving grace, too proud to pray to the God that made us![1]

What was true in 1863 is true today—America has become "too self-sufficient" for God. We have become "too proud to pray to the God that made us." But, as Lincoln also told Congress, prayer may be the only activity that can "nobly save…the last best, hope of earth."[2]

We must heed the wisdom of America's official national motto: "In God We Trust."

Yes, we need to advocate for just laws, vote for ethical politicians who will uphold the Constitution, defend the rights of the unborn, and guard our families against moral corruption. But to do these things without asking God to attend to our work is foolish, because it cuts us off from the greatest power in the universe.

James 5:16 says, "The effective prayer of a righteous [person] can accomplish much." So when we seek God's help and pray about the issues that affect our lives, we influence the fate of our families, our churches, and our nation. It has happened before in history, and it can happen again. The only thing keeping America from rising to its feet are Christian Americans who aren't yet falling on their knees.

That's why this book was written—to encourage you to ask God to bless America and to accomplish His perfect will in our nation. Each chapter of *Praying for America* features an inspiring story that demonstrates the power of faith in the life of our nation; a prayer you can use to lift up our families, our churches, and our country; and a passage of Scripture that will biblically ground your prayers.

When Jesus taught His disciples to pray in Matthew 6:5–13, He made it clear that the purpose of prayer is not to get our will done in heaven but to get God's will done on earth. And if ever there was a time when we needed God's will done in America, that time is now! Won't you join me in praying intently for the nation that we love?

For God's Will
to Be Done

In 1797—just fourteen years after America won independence from Britain, with the help of France—our relationship with France had deteriorated. The French Revolution had plunged that nation into godlessness. Churches were closed, crosses were forbidden, and Christian worship was outlawed. Hundreds of thousands were murdered in the name of "brotherhood."

France's new leaders seized American vessels and demanded millions of dollars in bribes to leave these ships alone. But America refused to pay these French terrorists.[1] This situation became known as the XYZ Affair, and it posed a great danger for the United States. As a new nation, we could not afford to lose ships, but we did not want to get mired in another war, either. With tensions mounting, President John Adams asked the retired George Washington to take charge of the army once again, and Washington agreed.

In July 1798, General Washington wrote to President Adams, placing the American cause in God's hands: "Satisfied, therefore, that you have sincerely wished and endeavored to avert war, and exhausted, to the last drop, the cup of reconciliation, we can, with pure hearts appeal to Heaven for the justice of our cause, and may confidently trust the final result to that kind Providence, which has heretofore and so often signally favored the people of these United States."[2]

President Adams chose to trust in God's will. On March 23, 1798, he declared a day of prayer and fasting. A year later, on March 6, 1799, Adams issued another proclamation for the nation to pray and seek God:

> I have thought proper to recommend...a day of solemn humiliation, fasting, and prayer; that the citizens on that day abstain, as far as may be from their secular occupation, devote the time to the sacred duties of religion, in public and in private; that they call to mind our numerous offenses against the most high God, confess them before Him with the sincerest penitence, implore His pardoning mercy, through the Great Mediator and Redeemer [Jesus], for our past transgressions, and that through the grace of His Holy Spirit, we may be disposed and enabled to yield a more suitable obedience to His righteous requisitions in time to come;...that He would make us deeply sensible, that "righteousness exalteth a nation but sin is a reproach to any people" [Proverbs 14:34].[3]

Many Americans did so, and they trusted God with the results. By God's mercy, war with France was avoided, and America thrived.

More than two hundred years later, our heavenly Father still has the whole world—including the United States of America—in His hands. While it's certainly true that we are facing crucial issues today, it's hardly the first time America has been in grave danger. Throughout our history, the United States has faced numerous threats, both from without and from within. Our Founding Fathers designed our system of government to withstand these threats.

But if we're not careful, we can give in to anxiety and worry. Every time a presidential election comes around, we hear statements like these from people across the political spectrum: "If so-and-so gets elected, our nation is doomed!" "This is the most important election of our lifetime!" "If that candidate wins, I'm leaving the country!" You may have even uttered a sentiment like this yourself.

We have a responsibility as believers to stand up, push back against evil, and influence the spiritual and moral direction of our country.[4] And the Bible encourages us to work hard for justice, God-honoring laws, and the spread of the gospel. But one thing Scripture says we should *not* do is worry. The apostle Paul put it this way in Philippians 4:6: "Be anxious for nothing, but in everything by prayer and supplication with thanksgiving let your requests be made known to God."

"Now, wait a minute," you might be protesting. "How is it possible not to worry when America is at a tipping point?"

First, we must do what we can to support God-honoring values, educate ourselves about the candidates, and participate in the voting process. We are to bring a Christian influence into our country. And one of the most powerful ways we can do that is through elections. When you cast a vote for a candidate, you are voting either for righteousness or unrighteousness.

Then, after you vote, trust in the sovereignty of God. Now, don't use God's sovereignty as an excuse for passivity in elections. Yes, God has ordained who is going to win the election, but He has also ordained the means by which that is going to come to pass—and it is through His people. You and I ought to be careful to maintain our witness during elections, never showing panic or fear or hatred toward others.

As Christians, God has called us to be salt and light in this decaying and darkening world. We are to pray for God's will to be done, participate in the political process, and then trust God with the results.[5]

⋆ ⋆ ⋆ A Prayer for America ⋆ ⋆ ⋆

Heavenly Father, thank You for being in control of the universe—including the United States and our elections. And thank You for giving me a say in who represents me in my government. Help me to fulfill that responsibility faithfully by voting in our elections. Whenever I am tempted to worry about the future of our nation, remind me of Your great love and provision. Forgive me when I give in to anxious thoughts instead of trusting You to work out Your purpose in America. May Your perfect will be done in all our elections. May the candidates seek after You and Your wisdom. And let me know if You desire for me to be one of those candidates. Bring revival to America before Your Son's return. Your kingdom come, Your will be done, on earth as it is done in heaven. In Jesus' name I pray. Amen.

⋆ ⋆ ⋆

Be anxious for nothing, but in everything by prayer
and supplication with thanksgiving let your requests
be made known to God. And the peace of God,
which surpasses all comprehension, will guard
your hearts and your minds in Christ Jesus.

—PHILIPPIANS 4:6–7

For Religious Freedom

In the early 1600s, every nation in Europe demanded loyalty to its state church, and England was no exception. Those who disagreed with the Anglican Church were harassed, fined, or jailed. But no Englishman could leave his country without permission. So, in 1608, one congregation of Separatists—as religious dissenters were known—uprooted their families and fled their homeland in secret, traveling across the English Channel to the Netherlands, which had recently become the first nation to grant religious toleration.

In the Netherlands, the Separatists enjoyed some measure of freedom. However, after eleven years, the situation began to change. Their work was hard, their children were abandoning their faith for the materialist Dutch culture, and war with Spain was looming on the horizon. If Spain conquered the Netherlands, then the Separatists would lose whatever religious freedom they had. In addition to all this, the small congregation was stopped from printing religious materials. They also desired to spread the gospel of Jesus Christ to new lands. So, after much prayer, the congregation decided to move again across the water, but this time much farther, to the brand-new English settlement of Virginia, in America.

Virginia stretched all the way up to New York at that time, and the Separatists figured they could settle there in peace—within English rule, but far enough removed to ensure religious freedom.

To procure supplies and passage, the Separatists had to become indentured servants to a shady investment company for seven years. Those who could afford to go purchased a small ship, the *Speedwell*, and set out for America on July 22, 1620. They had to make just one stop first, in England. There, the Pilgrims (as they now called themselves) met up with another small ship the investors had rented, the *Mayflower*, which would carry another group of Separatists and some Anglican colonists to the Virginia Colony.

After some underhanded dealings from the investors, both ships finally departed for America. But they had to turn back because the captain of the *Speedwell* said the ship was leaking. This happened a second time, and the captain declared the ship unseaworthy. Reluctantly, the passengers crammed together—Separatists and strangers alike—into the tiny *Mayflower*. Some families had to separate as the ship could not hold everyone.

At last, on September 6, 1620, the *Mayflower* set out alone across the vast Atlantic—a 150-foot-long boat stuffed with 102 passengers and 40 crew members, along with furniture, books, supplies, seed, livestock, and a new printing press.

Storms rocked the ship. At one point, the *Mayflower*'s main beam began to crack. If it broke, they would all die. Providentially, they had the printing press. They fitted its giant screw under the beam, cranked it up, and kept the ship from breaking apart.

It seemed that God was protecting them. But the storms blew the *Mayflower* far off course northward, all the way to Cape Cod, which they reached on November 11, after sixty-six days at sea. Because of poor winds, dangerous shoals, and the oncoming winter, they decided to settle on the Cape. Since they were now outside English territory, both Separatists and Anglicans signed a document known as the Mayflower Compact, which laid the foundation for the new colony's government.

The Mayflower Compact assured religious freedom. And God assured that this principle of freedom took root in the new land. When a landing party set out in a skiff to find a suitable settlement, a huge wave came out of nowhere. But instead of capsizing the boat, it deposited them gently on shore within sight of the ideal location: an abandoned native community that had plentiful water, a good harbor, cleared fields, a hill for defense, and buried corn and beans. They were saved from starvation! Even with this discovery, only half of the original passengers and crew survived that first harsh winter.

Over the next four months, the Pilgrims saw Native Americans only at a distance. Finally, on March 16, 1621, an Abenaki named Samoset walked into their town. "Welcome, Englishmen!" he said. The Pilgrims were stunned. Samoset had learned English from Anglo fishermen and traders. Later, Samoset brought another Native American who spoke even better English: Squanto.

Squanto had been abducted in 1614 from his Patuxet tribe by the English slaver Thomas Hunt and sold in Spain. There, he became a Christian and was freed by monks to travel to England. He learned English and found employment on a ship headed to America. But when he arrived back home in 1619, he found that his entire tribe had been wiped out by a three-year-long plague.

Squanto missed the plague but arrived back in time to help his new tribe of Pilgrims. He interpreted for them, arranged peace treaties, and taught them how to fish, hunt, and plant corn. He stayed with them until he died just a year later. Without Squanto's help, the Plymouth Colony likely would have perished.

To create a safe haven for religious freedom, God blew the Pilgrims 250 miles off course at just the right time so they would find two English-speaking Native Americans, one of whom was a fellow Christian! The Pilgrims rightly thanked God for Squanto.

They had struggled hard for religious freedom, and God had moved heaven and earth to ensure they got it.[1]

What about us? In America, we enjoy freedom of religion. But do we really value it? If we didn't have religious freedom, how far would we go to obtain it?

Our religious freedoms are being taken away at an alarming rate. God is not asking us to risk a dangerous journey across tumultuous seas to an unknown continent for the sake of our children. He simply wants us to pray—and fight—to keep what others have already won for us.

Pray that our religious liberties are protected in America. In addition to prayer, we can work through the legal channels to ensure that our nation's children inherit this same blessing. But even if we lose this freedom, pray that Christians in America stay committed to Jesus Christ.

In these last days before Christ's return, Christians will increasingly be challenged to stand against those who attempt to abrogate our constitutional rights and our biblical mandate to spread the message of Jesus Christ. But in doing so, we don't have to act like jerks. We must pick our battles carefully, be respectful of the governmental authorities that God has established, and be willing to suffer the consequences of our disobedience. Whatever happens, we need to be productive in the life God has given us, especially if we in America still have our hard-won religious freedom.[2]

★ ★ ★ A Prayer for America ★ ★ ★

Heavenly Father, You have called Americans to worship You in freedom. May I never take that privilege for granted. May I always remember the heavy price it took to gain that liberty. And may I use my freedom to offer thanksgiving to You and sacrificial love to others. I know that You are working all things together for the good of those who love You, whom

You have called according to Your purpose. Help me to believe that, no matter what I am going through. Thank You for loving me and giving me freedom. In Your name I pray, Lord Jesus. Amen.

★ ★ ★

You, my brothers and sisters, were called to be free.
But do not use your freedom to indulge the flesh;
rather, serve one another humbly in love.

—GALATIANS 5:13 NIV

3

For Truth to Prevail

When the Pilgrims lived in England and the Netherlands, their freedom of expression was routinely stifled. When they finally came to America, they brought only the essentials for survival—which included a giant printing press. That's how much they valued freedom of expression.

Throughout history, political tyrants have tried to promote only their viewpoint and silence any disagreement. The same still happens today in many parts of the world.

But our Founding Fathers valued freedom of expression so much that they included it as part of the First Amendment to the Constitution, along with freedom of religion, of assembly, and of petitioning the government. They knew that the free sharing of ideas kept people thinking and kept tyrants from suppressing the truth. This is why freedom of expression is one of our most cherished liberties today.

But it may not be for much longer. In America, freedom of expression is under attack. Instead of engaging in honest debate and allowing people to decide for themselves, many Americans label any views they disagree with as "hate speech" or "racist." They even try to pass laws that ban undefined "hate speech." And we are all aware of "fake news," in which media outlets engage in blatant bias and pretend it is honest reporting.

This destruction of dialogue is in full force on many of America's college campuses as well. Any discussion that faculties do not like is often labeled "hate speech," "microaggression," or "bigotry." Those with dissenting views have become the targets of open violence or have been expelled for not using a person's preferred pronouns.

But even this is not the biggest threat to our free speech. The biggest danger we face today comes from a tool that was meant to be the ultimate source for the open sharing of ideas: the internet. Today, a few gatekeepers—who were given special privileges by Congress as the new digital "neutral public forums" under section 230 of the Communications Decency Act of 1996—have now come to dominate the worldwide web. They no longer act as forums but rather as publishers who are immune from litigation for the material they publish or refuse to publish.[1] Let's examine just one of those gatekeepers as an example: Alphabet, Inc.

Now, you probably have never heard of Alphabet, Inc., even though it is one of the most powerful companies on earth.[2] You certainly have heard of at least two of the companies that Alphabet owns: Google and YouTube. Google is the number one site on the internet, and YouTube is the number two site.[3] A full 93 percent of Americans use Google to search the internet, and nearly 20 percent of all internet traffic is generated by YouTube. Nearly one billion people worldwide rely on Google every day.[4] You can see the power that Alphabet wields with just two of its many companies. People trust that Google, as a search engine, will help them find the news and views they are looking for.

But recent accusations against Alphabet are very disturbing.

Several senior engineers at Google admit that leadership at their company has a very left-leaning slant and that the search results they turn out are designed to give you what they want you to see and believe.[5] In other words, if you type in a controversial topic—say, "abortion"—then Google will give precedence to articles with their point of view. Opposing viewpoints appear way down the list, if at all.[6] In fact, Google recently included a "fact-checking" feature for search results that almost exclusively targeted conservative sites.[7]

Even Google's "autocomplete" program pushes their agenda. For instance, at the time of this writing, on Google's search page, if you start typing "men can" and then hit the space bar, Google autocompletes with "have babies," "get pregnant," "have babies now," "cook," "have periods," and "think about nothing." Likewise, if you type in "women can" and then hit the space bar, Google autocompletes with "fly," "vote," "do it," "do anything," and "be drafted." These suggestions do not reflect the most popular searches beginning with those words.[8] But Google wants you to think that they are. This is not speculation; it has been confirmed by internal documents and by programmers captured on insider videos.[9]

Speaking of insider videos, Google's sister company, YouTube, has banned those videos. In fact, YouTube has removed, shadow banned, or demonetized thousands of videos that express views that they do not like.[10] For example, YouTube placed G-rated educational videos about the Ten Commandments, the Korean War, and the formation of the nation of Israel on the "restricted list"—the same list as pornography.[11] This designation prohibits children in schools and libraries from viewing them. Members of Google's "transparency-and-ethics" group have also labeled Orthodox Jews Dennis Prager and Ben Shapiro as "Nazis."[12] Thousands more examples like this could be listed.

We could chalk up these designations to mistakes, except that these "mistakes" disproportionately happen to those on one side of the political spectrum.[13] And Google does not correct these designations even when confronted about them.[14] This is dangerous.

It is clear that this bias has a political motivation. Google executive Jen Gennai and senior Google engineers Zach Vorhies and Greg Coppola openly admit that Google's goal is to manipulate our political elections to one side.[15] And it has worked. Robert Epstein claimed that Google's one-sided influence on undecided voters in 2016 gave between 2.6 and 10.4 million extra votes to Hillary Clinton! This should alarm anyone, regardless of political persuasion.[16] Epstein voted for Hillary Clinton, but he values truth and free speech more than his preferred candidate getting into office. He worries that so much power over free speech—wielded by a handful of like-minded technology companies—will destroy our democratic process. As Dennis Prager testified before Congress on July 16, 2019, "Google and YouTube's (and for that matter Twitter and Facebook's) suppression of internet content on ideological grounds threatens the future of America more than any external enemy. In fact, never in American history has there been as strong a threat to freedom of speech as there is today."[17]

For our nation to survive in the internet era, Christians need to pray that Congress and the Justice Department break up technology monopolies and aggressively protect our free speech. You can also put pressure on your congressperson or senator to hold tech companies accountable for censoring speech, which is illegal under section 230 of the Communications Decency Act. Pray also that those who manipulate information and stifle free speech would repent.

You can also develop a healthy skepticism over anything you hear or read online. Realize that right now, most internet sites— even news or search sites—give you their perspective on the world, which may be true, partly true, or outright false. Check out alternative search websites, social media sites, and streaming video sites. And pray that your fellow Americans develop a healthy skepticism about what they hear or read online as well and that the truth prevails. American democracy depends on it.

★ ★ ★ A Prayer for America ★ ★ ★

Heavenly Father, I thank You that You are in control of every minute detail of this universe. Lord Jesus, You are the ultimate embodiment of truth. When You walked the earth, the rich and powerful tried to silence You because You spoke hard truths to them. They killed You, but they could not suppress the truth, for You rose again. Thank You, Lord, that truth will ultimately prevail. But that is no excuse for my complacency. You have called every Christian to stand up for the truth. In the short term, lies can do immense harm. Motivate Your people to stand for truth and free speech. Protect the free speech of every American and of every person worldwide. May honest debate and discussion happen freely. May we boldly speak the truth in love. And may those who suppress the truth repent before Your wrath comes upon them. In Your name I pray, Lord Jesus. Amen.

★ ★ ★

The wrath of God is revealed from heaven against
all ungodliness and unrighteousness of men
who suppress the truth in unrighteousness.

—Romans 1:18

4

For Protection
from Our Enemies

On December 7, 1941, at 7:48 a.m. local time, the Empire of Japan launched an unprovoked surprise attack on the US naval fleet stationed at Pearl Harbor, Hawaii. Before the day was over, the Japanese had killed over 2,400 innocent Americans and wounded another 1,143. Japan perpetrated this attack in an attempt to continue their brutal expansion over Southeast Asia and the Pacific. The Japanese had been taught that their emperor was a god and they were a chosen race, destined to rule inferior humans. This belief motivated them to perpetrate barbaric acts of brutality and aggression. The United States simply stood in the way of their advancing empire of blood.[1]

On another morning—September 11, 2001—radical Islamic terrorists hijacked four US airliners filled with fuel and crashed them, unprovoked, into the World Trade Center Twin Towers, the Pentagon, and a field in Pennsylvania. Their combined attacks killed almost three thousand innocent people and wounded another six thousand. The terrorists had been taught that America opposed

Allah's purposes and that killing themselves while killing Americans would please Allah and guarantee their place in heaven.[2]

At 9:02 a.m. Central Time on April 19, 1995, Timothy McVeigh, with the help of two accomplices, detonated a truck containing nearly five thousand pounds of homemade explosives in front of the Alfred P. Murrah Federal Building in Oklahoma City. The attack killed 168 innocent people (including 19 children) and injured more than 500 more. The men committed this terrible act of mass murder on the two-year anniversary of the fire at the Branch Davidian cult compound near Waco, Texas. The cultists had been in a standoff with federal agents for fifty-one days. McVeigh and his coconspirators believed the government had started the fire (a claim that was later debunked). The Waco siege occurred less than a year after another deadly standoff in Ruby Ridge, Idaho, which McVeigh also blamed on the government. McVeigh and his accomplices somehow thought that killing innocent adults and children would avenge what they saw as government overreach and would overthrow the authorities. They fancied themselves as heroes and believed that any act of violence they committed was justified.[3]

From foreign threats like radical Islamic terrorists, to cyber threats like the Chinese government, to domestic terrorist threats like Antifa, to people who are taught to hate our country or to disrespect authority, Americans share this world with many enemies who would harm us.

Why is so much hatred aimed toward America? For several reasons. We are not perfect, but many people want to destroy America because they are misguided. They have a skewed view of our nation and the world. They disproportionately focus on our faults to the exclusion of our many virtues. Others want to harm or destroy us so that they can become more powerful. Still others want to destroy us because we support Israel or because we are a nation built on Christian values. Whatever the reason, hatred for America abounds.

And we should not be surprised. America is a large, wealthy, and freedom-loving country. That makes us an equally large target for those who want to steal our wealth, use us as a scapegoat for their problems, or get us out of the way of their global plans.

All irrational hatred begins with evil desires and the lies of Satan. At root, it is a spiritual problem. And at the spiritual level, believers fight evil and falsehood with Christian love and gospel truth. However, even though the battle begins in the spiritual realm, it often extends into our physical world. When it does so, it threatens physical harm to us and to our countrymen. And we must oppose it.

If we didn't know the Lord, this dangerous world could paralyze us with fear. Thankfully, Romans 8:28 tells us that "God causes all things to work together for good to those who love God, to those who are called according to His purpose." That means Christians.

Even though God is in charge, that is no excuse for us to ignore threats to our nation. This principle goes all the way back to the Old Testament, to God's chosen people: Israel. God chose the Jews as His special possession. He loved His people, and He was in complete control of their circumstances. But Nehemiah 2:17–20 tells us that God still expected Nehemiah to build a wall around Jerusalem for protection.

As Christians, God loves us and has chosen us for salvation. But God has also called us to be responsible. We should take reasonable steps to protect our nation. That is why we have a military, intelligence agencies, and cybersecurity, and it is one reason we try to protect our border.

We must pray that God protects our nation from the very real enemies that threaten us. Ask God to give wisdom to America's leaders, so they will know how best to accomplish this goal. And pray for our military, border patrol, and intelligence agencies to do their jobs well.

As Jesus tells us in Matthew 5:44, we should love our enemies and pray for those who persecute us. Ask God to open their eyes to the truth before they face destruction. And pray for peace—both for your heart and for the world. Finally, pray for Christ's swift return, when He will implement His perfect peace on earth.

★ ★ ★ A Prayer for America ★ ★ ★

Heavenly Father, thank You for loving me and for sending Jesus to save me. And thank You that every detail of my life is in Your hands. Help me not to become complacent in Your love. Rather, let Your love motivate me to action. I want the best for my neighbors and countrymen. Protect us from those who want to harm us. Stop Satan from deceiving people into thinking that murdering Americans is somehow good. Give our leaders wisdom in how to protect us from all threats, both foreign and domestic. Help our military, border patrol, intelligence agencies, and cybersecurity experts to perform their jobs with skill and excellence. In Your name, Lord Jesus, I pray. Amen.

★ ★ ★

Deliver me from my enemies, O my God;
Set me securely on high away from those
who rise up against me.

—Psalm 59:1

For National Unity

In the 1950s, America had won the war against fascism. Our economy was booming, and so were our birth rates. But America still had an enemy: the Soviet Union. We were in a cold war with communism, which was spreading its oppressive godless philosophy from Eastern Europe to China, Korea, Cambodia, and Cuba. The Soviets' stated goal was to see the fall of all democratic capitalist societies—especially America—and the worldwide implementation of atheistic communism. The United States and the Soviet Union were rivals in almost every imaginable way.

Then, on October 4, 1957, the Soviets launched the *Sputnik* probe into Earth's orbit. The satellite circled Earth sixteen times a day. No one in America knew what this piece of machinery was capable of. All we knew was that the Russians had twenty thousand hydrogen bombs! Fear gripped many Americans. It seemed that the atheist slave-state was beating the land of the free. America had to do something. So, on May 25, 1961, President John F. Kennedy announced our goal of sending a man to the moon before the end of the decade. The space race had begun.

While NASA was steadily building our space program, America

began exploding with cultural changes. The 1960s turned out to be the most turbulent and divisive decade in America since the Civil War. In 1961, the Communists built the Berlin Wall, and in 1962, they placed nuclear warheads in Cuba, just ninety miles off our coast. President Kennedy was assassinated on November 22, 1963. As the decade wore on, Americans got entangled in Vietnam, the sexual revolution, and a general spirit of rebellion.

The chaos seemed to peak in 1968. On January 23 of that year, communist North Korea captured a US Navy vessel and held its crew hostage for eleven months. On January 30, the communist North Vietnamese launched the Tet Offensive, causing heavy US casualties. This caused support for the war—and for President Lyndon Johnson—to wane. Members of Johnson's own party began to challenge him, including John F. Kennedy's younger brother Robert Kennedy. On March 31, President Johnson announced that he would not seek a second term.

On April 4, Martin Luther King Jr. was assassinated. Waves of riots swept the nation, causing much damage and bloodshed. On June 5, Robert Kennedy was assassinated, and Alabama governor George Wallace entered the presidential race as an independent with the slogan "Segregation now, segregation tomorrow, segregation forever." This split the Democratic vote, leading to Nixon's victory.

Amid this cultural chaos, NASA's program continued unabated. From October 11 to 22, the *Apollo 7* mission orbited Earth, spending more time in space than all the Soviet flights to that time combined. Then, on December 21, the *Apollo 8* mission launched, carrying three astronauts to the moon. Their mission was to circle the moon ten times and then return. As they came around the moon on Christmas Eve, becoming the first humans ever to see Earth in its entirety, astronaut Bill Anders radioed back to the largest audience in history, "In the beginning, God created the heaven and the earth" (Gen. 1:1 KJV). The other astronauts then took turns reading from the first ten verses of Genesis.

A mere seven months later, on July 20, 1969, almost every person in America—204 million people, and millions more world-wide—listened live as Neil Armstrong and Buzz Aldrin descended to the moon. After the immortal words "the Eagle has landed" were spoken, the nation erupted with cheers. Aldrin then pulled out a chalice of wine and a wafer, and invited those back at mission control to join him as he became the first human to celebrate Christian Communion on another world.[1]

The moon landing united all Americans in a national pride and celebration not seen since World War II. Once again, we had a common cause, a common identity, and a common enemy that we had defeated.

Today, many people think unity in America is impossible. We are a diverse country with diverse worldviews. Many even believe that unity within the body of Christ is impossible. But Jesus calls Christians to unite. As believers, we share a common enemy—Satan—whom Jesus will one day vanquish. Ephesians 6:12 says, "Our struggle is not against flesh and blood, but against the rulers, against the powers, against the world forces of this darkness, against the spiritual forces of wickedness in the heavenly places."

As Christians, we all have one heavenly Father through our one Lord and Savior Jesus Christ, whom we celebrate with one faith and one baptism. And we are united in truth and love by one Holy Spirit in one goal of spreading Christ's kingdom. The apostle Paul put it this way in Ephesians 4:4–6: "There is one body and one Spirit, just as also you were called in one hope of your calling; one Lord, one faith, one baptism, one God and Father of all who is over all and through all and in all."

Jesus calls us to be united just as He and the Father are united. John 17:22–23 records His prayer for us: "that they [believers] may be one, just as We are one; I in them and You in Me, that they may be perfected in unity, so that the world may know that You sent Me, and loved them, even as You have loved Me."

As our nation seems to grow ever more divided, pray that Christians will unite in truth and love. Pray that in the essentials of the faith we show unity, in the nonessentials we show liberty, and that in all things we show charity. And pray that those around us see our example, come to saving faith, and extend that same spirit of love to others.

Pray also that God will bring unity to our divided nation. Ask God to silence those who strive to spread division and hatred and to bring any slanderers in the media to repentance. Learn how to engage in civil dialogue, especially with those with whom you disagree.

If Christians across America become united in spirit, love, and truth, then our nation will take notice, and Christ's kingdom will take off in unstoppable ways! Our nation will also benefit as divisions are healed and we together look to heaven for guidance.

⋆ ⋆ ⋆ A Prayer for America ⋆ ⋆ ⋆

Heavenly Father, our nation shares a common enemy, and it's not each other! Save us from Satan's divisive schemes. You call all Christians to live in unity. Even though we are all different, we have one Lord and Savior, Jesus Christ. Our love for our Christian brothers and sisters is a strong witness to the rest of the world that we are Your disciples. Forgive us when we argue over petty differences, and help us to restore our fellowship again. We can never compromise on sin, but we always strive for peace. Help us to be united in seeking first Your kingdom. And heal our divided nation. May we seek the welfare of our fellow citizens and engage in civil discourse with those with whom we disagree, and they with us. In Your name I pray, Lord Jesus. Amen.

★ ★ ★

He gave some as apostles, and some as prophets, and
some as evangelists, and some as pastors and teachers,
for the equipping of the saints for the work of service,
to the building up of the body of Christ; until we all
attain to the unity of the faith, and of the knowledge
of the Son of God, to a mature man, to the measure
of the stature which belongs to the fullness of Christ.

—EPHESIANS 4:11–13

For Fair Elections

In 1948, Lyndon Baines Johnson lost to former Texas governor Coke Stevenson in the Democratic primary for the Senate. The margin was about seventy thousand votes, but it was close enough to force a runoff. On the day of the runoff, Johnson still lagged behind by twenty thousand votes, with only San Antonio and a few other precincts left to report. Stevenson was not worried, however, since he had beaten Johnson in San Antonio's regular primary by a two-to-one margin. But when the runoff votes came in, Johnson had somehow beaten Stevenson in San Antonio by about ten thousand ballots. Later that evening, rural counties in the Rio Grande Valley cut Stevenson's lead to only 854.

The next day, an unknown precinct was miraculously discovered. Those votes went overwhelmingly to Johnson. But Stevenson still led by 349 votes by Tuesday. On Friday, election officials in the Rio Grande Valley made corrections in the election returns that cut Stevenson's lead to only 157. Later that same day, the tiny town of Alice, in Jim Wells County, sent in amended returns. In precinct 13, a box of votes was supposedly found with 202 additional votes in it. Of those, 200 were for Johnson. Only two went to Stevenson. Thus, six days after the polls had closed, Johnson had miraculously overcome a twenty-thousand-vote deficit. Of almost one million ballots cast, he had won by only eighty-seven.

Stevenson cried foul, and a federal district court ordered Johnson's name off the ballot of the general election until an investigation could take place. But that order was voided by Supreme Court justice Hugo Black at the request of Johnson's lawyer. The general election proceeded, and Johnson went on to beat the Republican candidate for the Senate seat. Johnson eventually went on to become vice president, and then president in 1963, when John F. Kennedy was assassinated in Dallas. Without his victory in 1948, it is doubtful that Johnson would have ever risen to the presidency.

For decades after, many were suspicious of Johnson's victory. However, no one could present conclusive proof that Johnson or his supporters had stolen the 1948 election. Finally, in 1977, Luis Salas, who had been an election judge in Jim Wells County during the 1948 election, confirmed what most people thought: Johnson's supporters had committed massive voter fraud. County officials had cast votes for absent voters, dead voters, and ineligible voters. For instance, in the infamous box 13 from Alice, Texas, the additional two hundred votes for Johnson were somehow cast in alphabetical order, in a different color ink from the other votes, and all in the exact same handwriting. In other instances, voting officials left the actual votes the same but changed the final numbers. In one precinct of Jim Wells County, someone had changed the 765 votes for Johnson to read 965 votes, thus instantly giving him an extra two hundred ballots. Lyndon Johnson had indeed stolen the election.

Attempts at voter fraud go all the way back to our nation's founding. The corrupt Tammany Hall organization in New York City, the political machine in Chicago, and disenfranchisement of black voters in Jim Crow South have all attempted to skew elections—and sometimes succeeded. Law-abiding citizens have continually fought against fraudsters over the decades to keep our elections legitimate.

Today, the threat of voter fraud is just as real. The Heritage Foundation has documented 1,177 proven cases of voter fraud, and Judicial Watch found that nine hundred thousand illegal aliens voted in the 2018 elections. In close elections, these frauds can decide an outcome. And in states without voter ID laws, the threat is that much greater.[1]

Our right to vote for who will represent us in our government is one of our most cherished privileges as citizens of the United States. It affirms the biblical concept that God has called every person to rule the world on His behalf: "God created man in His own image, in the image of God He created him; male and female He created them. God blessed them; and God said to them, 'Be fruitful and multiply, and fill the earth, and subdue it; and rule over the fish of the sea and over the birds of the sky and over every living thing that moves on the earth'" (Gen. 1:27–28). Although God alone gives this right, most governments through the ages have refused to acknowledge it. Today, Americans enjoy this right by the blood, sweat, and tears of those who fought for our freedom—both in our military and through courageous civil rights movements.

But this right exists only if our elections are kept fair and legitimate. The United States is powerful and wealthy. Such power and wealth attract those who would steal it by fraud. We must be ever vigilant against such thieves, and we must be good stewards of the blessings God has given to us. Pray that voter fraud is exposed, that voter registrars and election officials are upstanding and truthful, and that all of us watch for any attempted deceit. Report any suspicious activities you see to authorities, and consider applying to work at the polls in your next election. This is our nation, and God has called us to safeguard fairness in our election process.

★ ★ ★ A Prayer for America ★ ★ ★

Heavenly Father, You have called Your children to rule Your world with wisdom and integrity. You care very much that justice and honesty prevail in all circumstances. No matter is too small or too big for You. Our nation's forefathers fought and died so that we could live and worship in freedom. Help me to do my part to ensure that blessing for our nation's children and grandchildren. Please keep our country's elections fair and honest. Put the fear of You into the hearts of election officials. May election laws and results be honored and righteousness prevail as we look forward to Your future, perfect reign, Lord Jesus. In Your name I pray. Amen.

★ ★ ★

A just balance and scales belong to the LORD;
All the weights of the bag are His concern.

—PROVERBS 16:11

For Our President and Leaders in Washington, DC

Abraham Lincoln is considered by many to be America's greatest president. He faced a nation bitterly divided over slavery to the point of tearing in two. He had to deal not only with slavery but also with secession, Civil War, and civil rights. Looking back, we see that Lincoln maneuvered through this unimaginable pressure with wisdom, restraint, courage, and tact. And Lincoln is equally remembered for his amazing prose. Both of his inaugural addresses are masterpieces, and his Gettysburg Address is considered by many to be one of the greatest speeches ever given.

But you wouldn't know any of this while Lincoln was in office if you listened only to his critics. Naysayers eviscerated him every day. They attacked Lincoln's policies, his appearance, his heritage, his education, his speaking ability, his intelligence, his character, his family—nothing was off-limits. He was called a "yahoo," a "barbarian," "unshapely," an "idiot," a "coward," and "the original gorilla" (those last three insults came from his commanding general, George McClellan). One writer noted, "No matter what Lincoln did, it was never enough for one political faction, and too much for another.

Yes, his sure-footed leadership during this country's most-difficult days was accompanied by a fair amount of praise, but also by a steady stream of abuse—in editorials, speeches, journals, and private letters—from those *on his own side*, those dedicated to the very causes he so ably championed."[1]

For example, Elizabeth Cady Stanton—a leading abolitionist of the time—called Lincoln "Dishonest Abe" in 1864—amazingly, only a year after he signed the Emancipation Proclamation. She called his administration incapable and rotten, and she worked against his reelection. She swore that if Lincoln "is reelected I shall immediately leave the country."

Many of Lincoln's opponents ridiculed his speeches. One Pennsylvania newspaper reported about the Gettysburg Address, "We pass over the silly remarks of the President. For the credit of the nation we are willing that the veil of oblivion shall be dropped over them, and they shall be no more repeated or thought of." Likewise, a writer for the *London Times* opined, "Anything more dull and commonplace it wouldn't be easy to produce."

Sound familiar? Social media and cable news have nothing on these guys. Presidents—whether good or bad—face immense pressures few of us can imagine. And even the best American presidents are affected by smears. After reading one particularly vicious attack from a fellow abolitionist, Lincoln is reported to have said, "I would rather be dead than, as president, thus abused in the house of my friends."

What should you do if you love the current president? Pray for the president. What should you do if you despise the current president? Pray for the president. No matter who is in charge, we are commanded by God to pray for our leaders. Paul wrote, "I urge that entreaties and prayers, petitions and thanksgivings, be made on behalf of all men, for kings and all who are in authority" (1 Tim. 2:1–2).

When God inspired the apostle Paul to give this command, Rome was led by the wicked emperor Nero. This was the same Nero who sadistically murdered Christians and let Rome burn—both figuratively and literally. So Paul was urging Christians to pray for a national leader not only with whom they disagreed but also who was truly evil.

The truth is, we should pray for evil leaders even more than righteous ones—first, for their repentance and salvation, and second, that God would direct them to make righteous choices. For God can cause even evil leaders to make wise decisions. Proverbs 21:1 tells us, "The king's heart is like channels of water in the hand of the LORD; He turns it wherever He wishes."

And the president isn't the only leader in Washington, DC, for whom we should pray. The apostle Paul's command in 1 Timothy 2:2 to pray for "all who are in authority" also includes the vice president, nine Supreme Court justices, 15 cabinet heads, 17 district judges, 100 senators, 435 representatives, thousands of staffers, and tens of thousands of unelected bureaucrats who run agencies and remain in the capital for decades, regardless of who gets elected. Each of these people wields authority over us. They all are susceptible to temptation and corruption. And whether you agree or disagree with their politics, they all need our prayers.

★ ★ ★ A Prayer for America ★ ★ ★

Heavenly Father, Psalm 33:12 declares, "Blessed is the nation whose God is the LORD." I realize that You are not a respecter of people or nations. Any country that reverences You will be blessed by You. And any nation that rejects You and Your Word will be rejected by You. I pray for spiritual and emotional healing for America. I ask that You give the president, vice president, the cabinet, Congress, the courts, and federal agencies the wisdom and courage they need to lead our country wisely. Remind them that they work for the American people and that they will one day answer to You. For You are the ultimate Ruler and Judge. I pray this in Your name, Lord Jesus. Amen.[2]

★ ★ ★

I urge that entreaties and prayers, petitions and
thanksgivings, be made on behalf of all men, for kings
and all who are in authority, so that we may lead
a tranquil and quiet life in all godliness and dignity.

—1 TIMOTHY 2:1–2

For Our State
and Local Leaders

In 1783, General George Washington was wrapping up his successful military campaign against the British, but his troops were not happy. They had not been paid by the Continental Congress in quite some time, and they wanted to use their military might to threaten Congress with force. Some of Washington's officers even wanted to make America a monarchy and crown George Washington as their first king.

But Washington would have none of it. According to one historian, "Washington denounced the move as destructive of the very ground of republican government."[1]

What is a "republican government"? A republic is a form of government that acknowledges that political power comes from the people—not from military force or a monarch—and it should remain as close to the people as possible.

When King George III of England heard that Washington planned to step down after America gained its independence, he reportedly said, "If he does that, he will be the greatest man in the world."[2] And true to his word, when the revolution was over, Washington handed the power of the US Army back over to Congress.

Once the Constitution was ratified by the thirteen states in 1789, Washington was elected as our first president. He is the only president in our nation's history to win by a unanimous electoral college vote. The same thing happened again at his reelection. George Washington could have been reelected continuously for life if he had wanted. But he refused to seek a third term. Washington set an amazing precedent—a precedent followed for 150 years—that a single person should not hold that powerful of a position for very long.

Washington's actions exemplified the biblical values of the new republic. The Bible teaches that every person is royalty and has a part in ruling God's creation. But the Bible also teaches that when Adam and Eve fell, all their descendants fell with them. So, in Genesis 9:6, God set up civil government to punish evil. The Bible confirms in Romans 13:1–13 and in 1 Peter 2:13–17 that government still has this function today. Therefore, since the human heart is supremely evil, giving power to one person, unaccountable and far removed from the people, can breed corruption and tyranny. Even godly kings like David and Solomon can let power go to their heads, resulting in disaster. The Bible teaches that this problem of the human heart will persist until Christ returns.

Thankfully, our Founding Fathers were steeped in the Bible and in history. Many had experienced corrupt monarchs in Europe, and all had experienced the corruption of the English king. Their solution was brilliant: a federal constitutional democratic republic.

Let's look at what each part of this system entails. To honor the image of God in mankind, the Founding Fathers made our government a democracy: Every law-abiding adult votes. But to restrain the sin that lurks in every human heart, they established limitations on voting. First, we elect representatives to rule for us. A direct democracy can easily degrade into mob rule. Second, when electing the president, instead of simply counting all the votes, each state appoints electors to the electoral college, based on that state's popular vote, who then elect the president and vice president. This adds one more layer in our democracy, protecting us from mob rule. Third, we have the Constitution, which explicitly limits the power that the federal government can wield. Fourth, we divide power among three branches of government—with even the legislative branch divided into two houses—each with established checks and balances. And finally, our government is federal: There is a division between national, state, and local governments.[3]

In most nations around the world, and throughout most of history, authority trickled down from a monarch on top. But in the United States, authority ultimately rises from the bottom, from the people made in God's image. Thus, we were families before we were communities, we were communities before we were states, and we were states before we were a nation. Each region had to rule themselves before they were allowed into the larger entity. And once in, the states maintained most of their own autonomy.

In modern politics, we often forget about our state and local officials. This is tragic because our founders envisioned most of the power residing there. Each state is supposed to be its own small government that checks federal power. That is why our nation is called the United States of America. That is also why each state—regardless of population—is given two senators. The Senate helps balance the House of Representatives (which is based on population) and helps prevent a mobocracy.

State and local officials need our prayers just as much as our federal leaders in Washington, DC, do. First, pray that they make wise choices on behalf of us, their constituents. Second, pray that they accept the responsibilities of their position and not look immediately to the federal government to solve all their problems. Finally, ask God if He wants you to become more involved in local politics, or to even run for state or local office. Our nation needs godly people in every level of government.

⋆ ⋆ ⋆ A Prayer for America ⋆ ⋆ ⋆

Heavenly Father, give wisdom and courage to my local and state officials. May they govern with integrity and make laws that honor You. Thank You that I live in a country that was founded on biblical principles. Help me be a good steward of Your blessings and to live with wisdom, courage, and integrity, knowing that one day I will stand before You to give an account of how I stewarded Your blessings. And thank You, Lord Jesus, for saving me from my sins. In Your name I pray. Amen.

⋆ ⋆ ⋆

Every person is to be in subjection to the governing
authorities. For there is no authority except from
God, and those which exist are established by God.
Therefore whoever resists authority has opposed
the ordinance of God; and they who have opposed
will receive condemnation upon themselves.

—ROMANS 13:1–2

For Christians to Answer God's Call to Lead

Michael Dale "Mike" Huckabee was born in the small town of Hope, Arkansas, in 1955. His dad worked as a fireman and a mechanic, and his mom was a clerk at a local gas company. When Huckabee was fourteen, he got a job reading the news and weather for a local radio station. During high school, Huckabee also became involved in his church and in several youth political organizations. He was elected student council vice president and then student council president at Hope High School. He considered running for public office as an adult. *But could I win?* he wondered. He expected to have a career in broadcasting or communications and to use those skills for an evangelical organization. *I'll serve God in ministry,* he told himself. *Perhaps one day I'll be ready to run for office.*

In 1973, Huckabee graduated high school, becoming the first man in his family to do so. Not only that, but he went on to Ouachita Baptist University in Arkadelphia, Arkansas. He paid his own way, working forty hours a week at a radio station and delivering sermons on the weekends. He earned a four-year degree in two years and three months, "not because I was smarter than everyone else," he said, "but because I couldn't afford four years of that."[1] But he appreciated his undergraduate education because it cost him something.

He then went on to attend Southwestern Baptist Theological Seminary in Fort Worth, Texas, but he dropped out after a year to work for a local ministry. He became an ordained Baptist minister and spent the next twelve years faithfully serving churches in Pine Bluff, Arkansas, and Texarkana, Texas. He also started local television stations in both cities, producing documentaries, broadcasting football games, and hosting a show called *Positive Alternatives*.[2]

During his time as a pastor, Huckabee saw up close and personal how grand government policies, written hundreds of miles away, affected ordinary Americans in their everyday lives.[3] This experience profoundly impacted him. In 1989, Huckabee decided to run for office in his denomination and won. From 1989 to 1991, he served as president of the Arkansas Baptist Convention. Huckabee was beginning to see the need for Christians to run for public office in order to enact wise and righteous laws. "I could be the guy who always complained from the stands," he later recounted, "or I could suit up and offer myself to play the game."[4] So, in 1992, Huckabee ran for US Senate…and lost.

But he didn't give up. That same year, Arkansas governor Bill Clinton was elected president of the United States, and lieutenant governor Jim Guy Tucker took over the gubernatorial position. This created a vacancy for the lieutenant governorship, and a special election ensued in 1993. Huckabee had learned from his previous failed run and presented himself again with a wiser campaign, this time winning the special election. He beat the odds and became only the fourth Republican to hold statewide office in Arkansas since Reconstruction.

But the Democratic establishment in Little Rock (the state capital) was not happy about it.

The doors to my office were spitefully nailed shut from the inside, office furniture and equipment were removed, and the budget spent down to almost nothing prior to our arriving. After fifty-nine days of public outcry, the doors were finally opened for me to occupy the actual office I had been elected to hold two months earlier.[5]

Huckabee endured the harassment and came out more popular than before. He found a way to work with the most lopsided legislature in America and won reelection as lieutenant governor in 1994. In 1996, Jim Guy Tucker had to resign from governing Arkansas due to corruption involving the Whitewater scandal, and Huckabee became governor in 1996.

Huckabee won reelection in 1998 and again in 2002. Since he had served Arkansas's maximum of two consecutive four-year terms, his tenure ended in 2007. Huckabee ended up being the third-longest-serving governor in Arkansas history.[6]

Though Huckabee is not perfect (none of us is), and you may not agree with every policy decision he made, he tried to govern according to biblical principles, knowing that one day he would have to answer to God for them. During his time in public office, he was able to implement many godly and wise policies that benefited all Arkansans. "When people say what is the greatest thing you've ever accomplished," he said, "[it] is that when I finished the entire experience of lieutenant governor and governor…my kids, who I cherish a lot, did not reject everything I stood for."[7] Huckabee has become a voice for righteousness nationwide through radio and TV programs and through his continued political involvement.

Today, God is calling some of you to sacrifice some of your time to serve by running for public office. America is facing critical dangers, and He has put you in your specific time and place to effect great positive change as an elected official, either locally, statewide, or nationally.

Now, I know that many of you are reluctant to run for office. You may think that you could never win. But many non–career politicians have won elections in America, as Huckabee did.

Others of you may think that it is pointless or even sinful to try to enact righteous and wise laws. "We should focus only on the gospel," some of you have been taught. As well-intentioned as that thinking may be, it goes against Scripture. In Genesis 1:28, God blessed Adam and Eve and said to them, "Be fruitful and multiply, and fill the earth, and subdue it; and rule over the fish of the sea and over the birds of the sky and over every living thing that moves on the earth." This is the mission statement of mankind. We are made in God's image and are called to be fruitful, to subdue the earth, and to rule over it on God's behalf. Now, one way we do that is certainly through evangelism and discipleship: "Go therefore and make disciples of all the nations, baptizing them in the name of the Father and the Son and the Holy Spirit" (Matt. 28:19). But evangelism is not the only way. Many are also called to start families, create art, become professors, and, yes, enact just laws.

Many Christians have been wrongly taught to retreat into holy huddles and remove themselves from the arts, academia, and politics. But every area where Christians retreat from is taken over by Satan and false worldviews. On the contrary, God calls us to extend His influence into every area of life. In Matthew 6:10, Jesus taught Christians to pray: "Your kingdom come. Your will be done, on earth, as it is in heaven." If we pray to extend God's kingdom and will on earth, then we should work to extend it as well, not just through evangelism and personal holiness but also through involvement in our local, state, and federal governments—to be the righteous leaders our nation needs. Now, we know that God's will is only perfectly accomplished on earth when Christ returns. But that is no excuse not to follow God's will now.

The Bible declares—and the Constitution rightly recognizes—that every adult citizen of the United States is its leader because God commands us all to lead.[8] We cannot abdicate this responsibility.[9] Today, America is in crisis once again. Our nation needs godly men and women to lead—and God may be calling you to do it.

✷ ✷ ✷ A Prayer for America ✷ ✷ ✷

Heavenly Father, You created me in Your image, to fill, subdue, and rule Your world. Thank You that I live in a country that recognizes Your design that every person is royalty and that every person has the privilege—and the responsibility—to rule on Your behalf. Inform me if You want me to run for office or to support a godly candidate who will. May Your kingdom come and Your will be done, on earth, Lord, as it is done in heaven. In Your name I pray. Amen.

✷ ✷ ✷

God blessed them; and God said to them,
"Be fruitful and multiply, and fill the earth,
and subdue it; and rule over the fish of the sea
and over the birds of the sky and over every
living thing that moves on the earth."
—GENESIS 1:28

For Righteous Judges
and Justices

America's Founding Fathers wisely separated our federal government into three separate, coequal branches: the executive, legislative, and judiciary. They did this because they knew that the human heart is sinful and prone to corruption if given too much power. Separation of powers helps mitigate that problem. Also, giving specific functions of government to certain groups helps them focus on their task. The legislative branch writes the laws, the executive branch enforces the laws, and the judicial branch interprets the laws.

At least, that's how it's supposed to work in our nation. Most of the time, the Supreme Court and lower federal courts make decisions in accordance with the laws written by Congress and signed into law by the president that align with the Constitution. However, on occasion, a court forgets its role and tries to make laws from the bench. Alarmingly, this has been happening more frequently in recent decades. The Ninth Circuit is notorious for doing this, for example. The dangerous practice of judges legislating from the bench circumvents the power of the other branches of government. And while judges can be impeached, this hardly ever happens.

Thankfully, most of the time, the Supreme Court overrules the unconstitutional decisions of lower courts. But not always. Several times in our past, US justices have made decisions that caused dire consequences for our nation.

For example, in 1857, *Dred Scott v. Sandford* came before the Supreme Court. Dred Scott was a slave who was bought by army surgeon John Emerson. Emerson took Scott with him to Illinois (a free state) and Wisconsin (a free territory) before returning to the slave state of Missouri. Under the Missouri Compromise of 1820, any territory north of latitude 36°30' that was not already a slave state would be free. After Emerson died, Scott sued, saying that since he had been taken into free US territory, he had automatically been freed and was legally no longer a slave.

But in a seven-to-two ruling, the Supreme Court declared that Dred Scott could not be freed because he was not a person under the US Constitution. It therefore declared that the Missouri Compromise was unconstitutional. Chief Justice Roger B. Taney declared that no black person—free or slave—could ever claim US citizenship.

This ruling was an outrage for several reasons. Many black people were already living as free citizens in the North (and even some in the South). These Americans would be stripped of their citizenship. It also imposed a blatantly racist interpretation onto the US Constitution. The court basically said the Declaration of Independence was wrong when it affirmed that "all men are created equal" and "are endowed by their Creator with certain unalienable rights, that among these are Life, Liberty and the pursuit of Happiness." Instead, the Supreme Court stripped an entire group of people—made in the image of God—of their rights and dignities.

This convoluted Supreme Court ruling also overturned duly passed laws by Congress and the president. The *Dred Scott* decision contributed to a bloody civil war and prolonged the terrors of slavery. Thankfully, people fought back and reversed this precedent.[1] Under the Thirteenth, Fourteenth, and Fifteenth Amendments to the Constitution, black Americans were finally given their rights as citizens of the United States—but not before we lost 620,000 Americans in our deadliest war.[2]

Americans must remain vigilant to prevent this kind of tragedy from happening again by ensuring that our government functions according to its design. Today, there are two very different schools of thought among our nation's judges about how to view the Constitution. One is the constructionist viewpoint of the Constitution. Constructionists believe that judges have the responsibility to abide by the original intent of the framers of the Constitution. Even though we live in a rapidly changing world, we are still to look to the principles found in the Constitution to make decisions. The only way those principles can be altered is by the intentionally laborious process the Founding Fathers devised for amending the Constitution. This is our bedrock, and it prevents judges from becoming tyrants. That is the constructionist viewpoint.

However, a growing number of judges have adopted the expansionist view of the Constitution. Expansionists believe that the Constitution is an ever-changing body of truth. One observer said it this way: "It's as if the Founding Fathers wrote the Constitution on a blackboard and gave judges both an eraser and a piece of chalk." The result of this expansionist view of the Constitution is that the judiciary is granting imaginary rights to some individuals while at the same time erasing the very real rights of other individuals.

Many Americans assume the federal government has the final say in every legal issue. But nothing could be further from the truth!

The framers of the Constitution never envisioned such sweeping authority for the federal government. The Tenth Amendment of our Constitution reads, "The powers not delegated to the United States by the Constitution, nor prohibited by it to the States, are reserved to the States respectively, or to the people." In other words, the only power the federal government has are those powers that are found in the Constitution. The rest of the power belongs to the states and to the people. That is why it is so important that before we elect people to office, we know their view of the Constitution.[3]

The era of the judges in Israel's history was terrible and lawless. Judges 21:25 says, "There was no king in Israel; everyone did what was right in his own eyes." Today, we are living in a new era of judges who acknowledge no authority as king above themselves and do whatever is right in their own subjective eyes. Pray for our judges and justices, that they will rule according to constitutional law, not according to their own whims.

Isaiah 10:1 says, "Woe to those who enact evil statutes and to those who constantly record unjust decisions." Pray that our nation removes bad judges and confirms good jurists. This is necessary for a just society, for God hates injustice.

★ ★ ★ A Prayer for America ★ ★ ★

Heavenly Father, You have made Your Son, the Lord Jesus Christ, the Supreme Judge, Lawgiver, and King of the universe. And Your Word says that one day, He will render judgment on every one of us. You love when judges rule according to justice and equity but hate when they rule corruptly. Give our nation's judges and justices wisdom in discerning cases, and give them a fear of You to make the right choice. Remind them that the Constitution is their duly established authority, and every legitimate authority comes from You. Help them understand that they will one day have to answer to You, Lord Jesus, for every ruling they make. Give wisdom to our president and Senate to choose and confirm wise and righteous judges. In Jesus' name I pray. Amen.

★ ★ ★

You shall do no injustice in judgment; you shall not
be partial to the poor nor defer to the great,
but you are to judge your neighbor fairly.

—LEVITICUS 19:15

For Our Troops

If you are living in freedom anywhere on earth today, it is because of the United States military.

If you think I'm exaggerating, then consider these examples: In World War II, the American military played a key role in stopping the Nazis and their allies from imposing their brutal reign far and wide. In the Cold War, Korean War, and Vietnam War, American troops stopped the Soviet socialists and Chinese communists from taking over the world. And in recent years, the American military has fought back radical Islamic terrorists who have attacked the West. The United States has continually protected people all over the world from losing their freedom.

Now, it's important to understand that our nation does not seek out conflict, but when evil rears its ugly head, we must oppose it. Such a struggle takes its toll on our troops. But thankfully, ever since America's founding, we have been blessed with military leaders who knew we needed God's help. From George Washington seeking divine providence, to US presidents and Congresses calling for days of fasting and prayer, to World War II chaplains praying for good weather, America has a long history of relying on God's mercy and aid.

Nowhere was this seen more clearly than in August 1776. British troops who had been expelled from Boston turned their attention to taking New York City. In response, General George Washington moved his army to New York. Morale was high in the colonies, and the Continental Army swelled to almost twenty thousand volunteers.

However, it wasn't long before hundreds of British ships filled New York's harbor, bringing thirty-two thousand soldiers. It was the largest invasion force the world had ever seen. Washington's formerly chipper troops began to worry. The entire American army was located on the adjacent islands of Manhattan and Long Island. If either was taken, America would lose the war and independence. Many Americans would be hanged as traitors.

In response, the Continental Congress ordered May 17, 1776, to be a day of "humiliation, fasting and prayer" throughout the colonies. They urged citizens to "confess and bewail our manifold sins and transgressions, and by a sincere repentance and amendment of life, appease his [God's] righteous displeasure, and through the merits and mediation of Jesus Christ, obtain his pardon and forgiveness."[1] George Washington shared this order with his troops and commanded "all officers and soldiers to…incline the Lord and Giver of victory to prosper their arms."[2]

On July 9, a copy of the newly passed Declaration of Independence was delivered to General Washington. He had it read aloud to his troops. There was no going back now. Motivated, his army hunkered down for the fight.

In this first battle after independence was declared, it seemed as if God had rejected their prayers. The British landed on Long Island on August 22, and five days later, they made a frontal attack on American's position, as Washington had expected. However, a loyalist traitor had led ten thousand redcoats through the night to make a surprise attack on the Continental Army from behind. The

Americans were flanked! The Americans suffered about a thousand casualties that day.[3]

Then miracles began to happen. For some inexplicable reason, the British commander did not press his attack but stopped before the Americans were completely defeated. This allowed Washington to order a retreat by ferrying the remaining troops from Long Island across the East River to Manhattan. This was extremely risky. However, although the sea was choppy where the British ships were located, it was remarkably calm in the East River.

So, on the night of August 28, Washington began to transport men, cannons, and horses across under cover of darkness. As the sun began to rise on August 29, half the American troops were either still on the river or on Long Island. But then an unusual—and extremely unseasonable—fog descended over the American and British encampments. When the fog finally lifted, nine thousand American soldiers had safely evacuated without losing a single person. This was one of the greatest acts of military evacuation in history.[4] Had the Americans not been able to retreat, the war would have been over.

Never again was the entire Continental Army located in one location for capture. God had answered their prayers, and the Americans eventually went on to victory.[5]

Today—as always—we must rely on God's help. Pray for wisdom for our military leadership. Pray for our troops going into battle, that God will fill them with skill, courage, and joy. Pray for their safety. Pray for their families from whom they are separated and whom they are not sure if they will see again. Maybe reach out to a family whose loved one is deployed and invite them to church and be a friend to them. Ask God if He wants you to donate to worthy causes, such as the Fisher House Foundation, the Semper Fi Fund, or the Wounded Warriors Family Support organization.

Consider visiting wounded servicemembers if you live close to a Veterans Affairs hospital.

If you are currently serving in our military, thank you. We appreciate your service more than you know. Trust in Jesus as your Savior and ultimate General. Find a group of believers wherever you are, and meet with your chaplain if possible. Remember, God is your Shield and Protector, and He is with you wherever you go.

★ ★ ★ A Prayer for America ★ ★ ★

Heavenly Father, thank You for intervening many times on America's behalf throughout our military history. Thank You for the brave men and women who have served our country and who continue to serve today. Give them skill for waging righteous warfare. They face hardships and sacrifices for us every day. Give them joy, wisdom, and courage. Provide godly chaplains who will boldly preach Your Word and minister to spiritual needs. Most of all, grant them conviction of sins and faith in Jesus Christ as their Lord and Savior. Reassure them that You are with them in battle. And let them know that my fellow citizens and I love them, support them, and are praying for them. In Jesus' name I pray. Amen.

★ ★ ★

Blessed be the LORD, my rock,
Who trains my hands for war,
And my fingers for battle.
—PSALM 144:1

For Law Enforcement

The American West was won by legendary lawmen like Wyatt Earp, John Hughes, and Frank Hamer. One heroic marshal was even part of the inspiration for the Lone Ranger, although he has often been overlooked. His name was Bass Reeves.

Reeves was born into slavery in Arkansas, in July 1838. When the Civil War broke out, his owner, William Steele Reeves, let his son George take him into battle with him. However, Reeves ran away to the Indian Territory (later Oklahoma), where he hid among the Native Americans. While there, he learned Native American languages, customs, and tracking skills. Reeves also became a dead shot with firearms.

After the Thirteenth Amendment was passed in 1865, Reeves was no longer considered a runaway slave, so he moved back to Arkansas, where he bought some land. A year later he married Nellie Jennie, with whom he had ten children. Reeves became a successful farmer, rancher, and occasional scout for the US marshals who needed to travel into Indian Territory. That area had become increasingly lawless as desperados took refuge in the territory. So, in 1875, US marshal James Fagan was tasked to lead two hundred deputies to clean up the lawless land. Fagan heard of

Reeves and recruited him to be the first black US deputy west of the Mississippi.

Working with other legendary lawmen, Bass Reeves patrolled over seventy-five thousand square miles—the largest jurisdiction in the United States—on his huge white stallion. He could neither read nor write, so before he went out on patrol, Reeves had someone read to him the warrants, each of which he would memorize. He was courageous, imposing, and tenacious but also polite and stylish.

And he was also great at undercover police work. When need arose, Reeves would pose as a cowboy, gunslinger, grifter, farmer, or even as an outlaw. He always wore two Colt Peacemaker pistols. Reeves was ambidextrous and rarely missed his first shot. He was never wounded, although his hat and belt were shot off on separate occasions. He is credited with more than three thousand arrests during his thirty-four-year career. And Bass Reeves always left a silver dollar as his calling card.[1]

This is the stuff of legends. But did you know that members of law enforcement are also ministers of God? That's right. God's Word says,

> Every person is to be in subjection to the governing authorities. For there is no authority except from God, and those which exist are established by God. Therefore whoever resists authority has opposed the ordinance of God; and they who have opposed will receive condemnation upon themselves… for it is a minister of God to you for good. But if you do what is evil, be afraid; for it does not bear the sword for nothing; for it is a minister of God, an avenger who brings wrath on the one who practices evil. (Rom. 13:1–2, 4)

Police officers, judges, border patrol agents, ICE agents, and other federal officers of the law are not perfect. But they are all part of law enforcement that God has ordained and therefore must be respected and obeyed.[2] We should pray for them and thank them for risking their lives for our safety every day.

God has also given civil authorities the right to use lethal force if needed. The apostle Paul tells us in Romans 13:4 that civil authority "does not bear the sword for nothing; for it is a minister of God, an avenger who brings wrath on the one who practices evil."[3] In Paul's day, the Roman authorities used the sword for three things: to defend the Roman borders against invaders, to defend themselves, and to behead Roman citizens who had been convicted of capital crimes. Now, as Luke 22:36–38 makes clear, everyone has the right to defend themselves or someone else from a violent attack. But the civil government is the only institution in the present Church Age (the period of time from Pentecost until the Rapture) that God has given the right to use lethal force to secure national borders or to avenge innocent life. God has ordained families, but parents cannot kill their children. And God established the church, but the church has no right to execute anyone.

Of course, members of law enforcement are people, too, so we can find a corrupt or incompetent cop, judge, or federal agent every now and then. But that does not mean that we disrespect all law officers. Romans 13:5 states, "It is necessary to be in subjection [to civil authorities], not only because of wrath, but also for conscience' sake." We obey law enforcement to avoid punishment and to keep a clear conscience. Instead of blanket rebellion, we should prosecute the bad apples on a case-by-case basis, just as we would prosecute a corrupt pastor or corrupt parent on an individual basis. But we are not to disrespect all pastors, parents, or peace officers. My brother Tim was a police officer for many years, so this issue is not just theoretical to me. I have seen firsthand what law enforcement has to deal with.

To honor God, we must obey law enforcement. In fact, the

only time to disobey a law or civil authority is if they are forcing you to do something sinful. Then you should disobey, as Daniel did in Daniel 6:5–10, or as the early Christians did in Acts 4:18–31. In such cases, you have an obligation to a higher authority. You may incur a penalty for such disobedience, but you would be suffering for righteousness' sake. And Jesus said in Matthew 5:10, "Blessed are those who have been persecuted for the sake of righteousness, for theirs is the kingdom of heaven."[4]

But in any other instance, we must obey law enforcement. And we should pray for them: for their safety, courage, and wisdom. Finally, we should thank them for performing the difficult job they have to do. God expects us to do nothing less for His ministers.

★ ★ ★   **A Prayer for America**   ★ ★ ★

Heavenly Father, thank You for our nation's police officers, judges, border patrol agents, ICE agents, and intelligence officers who restrain evil and keep us safe. They perform an often dangerous and thankless job. I thank You for them, Lord, and I do not take them for granted. Give them courage, strength, protection, resources, and wisdom. May they see their jobs as being Your ordained ministers for our good. I look forward to the day when You will crush all evil under Your foot forever, and our legal system will no longer be necessary. Until then, I obey it as an act of worship to You. It's in Your name I pray, Lord Jesus. Amen.

★ ★ ★

It [civil government] does not bear the sword
for nothing; for it is a minister of God, an avenger
who brings wrath on the one who practices evil.

—ROMANS 13:4

For First Responders

On September 11, 2001, nineteen radical Islamic terrorists associated with the jihadi group al-Qaeda hijacked four airplanes in a coordinated suicide attack on the United States. They chose flights headed cross-country from the northeastern United States to California so that the planes would be filled with explosive fuel.

American Airlines Flight 77 was commandeered and flown into the Pentagon, killing 125 personnel and all 64 passengers on board. United Flight 93 was headed to another target, possibly the White House, the Capitol, or a nuclear power plant on the East Coast. The flight was delayed, so passengers onboard received calls about the other attacks. Realizing what was happening, a group of passengers heroically rushed the cockpit, attacked the terrorists, and caused the plane to crash into a field in Pennsylvania. All 44 passengers aboard died, but they prevented a much worse catastrophe on the ground.[1]

But the most dramatic and devastating of the attacks occurred at the World Trade Center Twin Towers in New York City. At 8:46 that morning, American Airlines Flight 11—a Boeing 767 carrying 20,000 pounds of jet fuel—crashed into the North Tower. Eighteen minutes later, another Boeing 767, United Airlines Flight 175, was flown into the South Tower.

Within seconds, thousands of firefighters, police officers, paramedics, and emergency medical technicians rushed into action. As people fled from the two burning structures, these first responders rushed into the buildings to rescue and treat any survivors they could find. However, at 9:59 a.m., the South Tower collapsed. Thirty minutes later, the North Tower fell. Only six people in the towers at the time of their collapse survived. In all, nearly three thousand people were murdered in the 9/11 attacks, 2,763 at the World Trade Center alone.

Of those casualties, 412 were first responders who gave their lives trying to rescue the wounded and trapped from that despicable act of evil. Two thousand first responders were injured, and thousands more were exposed to toxic dust from the wreckage.

Among those who died that day was the commissioner of the Fire Department of New York (FDNY), William M. Feehan. Even as a young man, Feehan decided to serve. He joined the United States Army during the Korean War and fought in active ground combat there on the peninsula. After serving with distinction, he was accepted into the FDNY. Feehan was the first firefighter in the FDNY to hold every rank, starting with the lowly probationary firefighter in October 1959. He served faithfully over the decades, until he eventually rose to the rank of deputy fire commissioner in 1992. He briefly served as acting fire commissioner in 1993 and 1994 until mayor Rudy Giuliani took office and could fill the position, at which time Feehan returned to being the deputy commissioner.

Normally, high-ranking members of New York City departments are asked to step aside so incoming mayors can make their own appointments. However, nobody asked Feehan to step aside from being the deputy commissioner. His knowledge and expertise were legendary. Rumor had it that he knew the location of every fire hydrant in the city.

On the morning of September 11, 2001, Feehan rushed to the scene at the World Trade Center to help, like the rest of his firefighters. His body was later found among the wreckage by a search-and-rescue K-9 unit. He had died eighteen days shy of his seventy-second birthday. Feehan was survived by four children and six grandchildren. His name is located on panel S-18 of the south pool of the National September 11 Memorial, at Ground Zero in New York City.[2]

Jesus said in John 15:13, "Greater love has no one than this, that one lay down his life for his friends." These first responders gave up their lives not for friends but for total strangers. Firefighters, paramedics, police officers, and emergency medical technicians are our lifelines in the worst of times. They are the first to arrive on the scene of a disaster—be it man-made or natural. They often self-lessly step into danger for the love of their fellow men and women. They often only have seconds to evaluate a situation and make critical decisions. Their skill and courage under fire save countless lives every day. We should never take them for granted.

Mark 10:43 says, "Whoever wishes to become great among you shall be your servant." These first responders have truly become great by the service they provide for all of us. If you see a firefighter, police officer, paramedic, or emergency medical technician, thank them for their heroic work. Pray that God gives them wisdom, courage, and a level head for the difficult situations they are faced with on a regular basis. Pray that they get all of the resources they need to perform their jobs with excellence. And be an advocate for them in your local community. They often face nit-picking scrutiny from opportunistic politicians and from misguided activists.

If you are a first responder, thank you. We love and appreciate what you do for us every day. We are praying for you. Your jobs are high in stress, so be sure to stay connected to God through His Son, Jesus Christ. Draw strength from His Word (the Bible), from His people (the church), and from Him directly, through prayer.

★ ★ ★ A Prayer for America ★ ★ ★

Heavenly Father, thank You for calling brave men and women to serve as first responders in the worst of moments. Please give all our police officers, firefighters, paramedics, and other emergency personnel wisdom, courage, training, protection, and the resources they need to conduct their jobs with excellence. Help me to respect them as they deserve. Bless their families, and give them Your peace. And help me to honor those who lost their lives in the line of duty. These men and women serve with greatness. I ask this in the name of Your Son, who served us to the point of death on a cross: our Lord and Savior, Jesus Christ. In His name I pray. Amen.

★ ★ ★

I am the LORD your God,
who upholds your right hand,
Who says to you,
"Do not fear, I will help you."
—ISAIAH 41:13

For Our Debt Problems

For years, experts warned about the dangers that faced New Orleans. Much of the city sits below sea level and is surrounded by levees—some of which had been woefully underengineered. In addition, eroding wetlands removed a valuable buffer to sea surges that would result if a major hurricane ever hit the area.

On one side of New Orleans sat the levees protecting the city from Lake Pontchartrain. These were particularly vulnerable. "We can start thinking about how can we reduce the amount of water that flows into Lake Pontchartrain and then floods the city," hurricane expert Ivor van Heerden advised in October 2004. But neither local nor federal officials paid much attention to him. "We had a number of officials who basically scoffed at us when we were talking about the potential of levees going and the very real threat to New Orleans of a major hurricane," he said a year later. "I think they just believed it wouldn't happen."[1]

But on August 29, 2005, it did happen. Hurricane Katrina, a category 3 hurricane, barreled into the Big Easy. Meteorologists and local officials ordered evacuations. But tens of thousands either stayed put or were unable to leave. On August 30, the Industrial

Canal breached, and water poured into neighborhoods. More levees soon gave way, resulting in a catastrophe.

Katrina resulted in the third most deadly—and the most expensive—natural disaster in US history up to that point. It cost $250 billion and is estimated to have taken the lives of 1,830 people. Hundreds of thousands more were left homeless.[2]

As bad as Hurricane Katrina was, we Americans are facing an even worse possible disaster today. Like waters building behind a levee, our debt level is rising as we continue to accumulate more and more debt, both personal and national.

At the federal level, as of the time of writing, our national debt sits at $23 trillion. As long as America's economy continues to grow, this poses no problem. However, no economy stays vibrant forever. Once we hit an economic downturn, the levee could break, and America could go underwater in bankruptcy. And the problem is not revenue. We are experiencing record-breaking tax receipts. The problem is that we are spending far more than we make.

This overspending is occurring at state, local, and personal levels as well. A 2019 report showed that sixty-three of America's seventy-five largest cities are broke. Several states are near insolvency, and consumer debt now exceeds $4 trillion, of which $1.5 trillion is student loans. Now, according to the Bible, it's not always wrong to go into debt. But it is wrong to accumulate debt if you don't have a sure means with which to repay it.[3]

Many people want student loan forgiveness. But this places the bill for their education on the backs of all Americans, two-thirds of whom do not have a college degree themselves. Plus, Psalm 37:21 states that such an action would be wicked: "The wicked borrows and does not pay back."

Raising taxes exorbitantly on the wealthy will not solve our national debt, either. The great Winston Churchill once said, "A country which tries to tax itself into prosperity is like a man standing in a bucket and endeavouring to lift himself up by the handle."[4] Besides, just because someone has more wealth than you does not give the government the right to take it away from them. We need to guard against the sin of coveting.

Today, many politicians—and many individuals with high debt—are seeking short-term gains in exchange for long-term destruction. We will mortgage America's future generations for our immediate comforts if we do not learn to manage our nation's debt. The wisest man who ever lived, King Solomon, put it this way: "The rich rules over the poor, and the borrower becomes the lender's slave" (Prov. 22:7) and "A good man leaves an inheritance to his children's children, and the wealth of the sinner is stored up for the righteous" (Prov. 13:22).

So, what is the solution to America's debt problems? The answer is the same regardless of whether the debt is personal, city, state, or federal: We must spend less than we bring in and pay down the debt with our surplus.

This is basic financial strategy, but many people today have gotten away from the basics. The Bible states, "There is precious treasure and oil in the dwelling of the wise, but a foolish man swallows it up" (Prov. 21:20). Living within our means requires maturity and delayed gratification. The apostle Paul demonstrated this attitude in Philippians 4:11: "Not that I speak from want, for I have learned to be content in whatever circumstances I am."

At the federal level, it will require politicians to put national interests before reelection chances and make tough decisions to cut unnecessary agencies and spending or to adjust the age when some people receive entitlements.

Pray that our nation's leaders will put the well-being of our children and grandchildren ahead of their own short-term political reelections. And pray that God gives them wisdom on how best to do this. Pray the same for our state and local government officials.

On the personal side, make sure that you are not accumulating debt that you have no means to pay back. If overspending is a temptation for you, then ask God to teach you contentment and wisdom. If you are drowning in debt, you can seek help by enrolling in a debt-elimination program, such as Dave Ramsey's Financial Peace University.[5]

Whatever the situation, be it personal, local, or national, we must spend less than we make, and we must pay down our debt. And we must do it fast. The water is rising, and a day of reckoning is coming when the levee will break.

★ ★ ★ **A Prayer for America** ★ ★ ★

Heavenly Father, teach me contentment and self-control. Forgive me when I ignore your wisdom, which You so generously give. Help me act responsibly and face the problems before me with courage and urgency. May I not pass off my financial responsibilities to my children and grandchildren. Help me to be disciplined and pay down my debts. Give our nation's leaders courage, wisdom, and a holy fear of You to make the tough decisions that reduce our expenses before the national debt crushes the next generation. And thank You, Lord Jesus, for taking my sin debt upon Yourself and paying it on the cross. Just like ocean levels during Hurricane Katrina, and our nation's increasing financial burden, my sin debt against You was always increasing. Thank You for paying that debt for me, Lord Jesus. Teach me to live responsibly as a good steward of all You have given me. In Your name I pray. Amen.

★ ★ ★

There is precious treasure and oil
in the dwelling of the wise,
But a foolish man swallows it up.

—PROVERBS 21:20

For Education

Let me tell you about an educational miracle. In a primitive society that had no running water, electricity, sewers, or paved roads—a society that was not even two hundred years old—the literacy rate was nearly 90 percent, one of the highest of any people in the history of the world! Where was this amazing place? It was colonial New England.[1]

New England had a higher literacy rate than the great nations of Europe. And they accomplished this feat without any centralized public schools, departments of education, massive government funding, teachers' unions, or computers. How was that possible?

It all came down to purpose. The Puritans who settled New England didn't seek literacy merely for literacy's sake. Nor was it even to succeed materially in the world, although that was a part of it. No, to them, knowing how to read and write was a means to a specific end: "Love the LORD your God with all your heart and with all your soul and with all your strength" (Deut. 6:5 NIV). The Puritans believed that a thorough knowledge of the Bible was essential for knowing God and living wisely. And they believed that every person needed to study God's Word for themselves.

These Puritan parents did not rely on the government to teach their children. They knew that they were responsible for the spiritual training of their own offspring. God has given this responsibility to every parent: "These commandments that I give you today are to be on your hearts. Impress them on your children. Talk about them when you sit at home and when you walk along the road, when you lie down and when you get up. Tie them as symbols on your hands and bind them on your foreheads. Write them on the doorframes of your houses and on your gates" (Deut. 6:6–9 NIV). God's Word is supposed to permeate our entire lives. That is what education is: loving God with all our minds.

All knowledge and learning should help us "to glorify God, and to enjoy him forever," as the Westminster Catechism says.[2] Even though we have institutionalized education in America today, and we pay professional teachers and administrators, God still holds parents primarily responsible for sharing the gospel with their children and wisely training them. While different parents choose different means to accomplish that goal—through public schools, private schools, charter schools, home schooling, and so forth—all parents are tasked with making sure their children receive training to love God, to love others, and to live a fruitful and fulfilling life to the glory of God.

However, many parents today believe that it is solely the state's responsibility to train their children. They send their youngsters to government-run schools for six or seven hours a day to be instructed by someone else, without ever checking what that person is instilling in them. And if parents seek any spiritual training for their kids at all, they may take their children to church once or twice a week and expect church leaders to teach them everything they should know about God and the Bible without discussing spiritual matters at home.

Now, spiritual training at church is important, and there is absolutely nothing wrong with public education. But these times of teaching should supplement what parents are already instilling in their children. If you are a parent, you must ensure that your children receive the proper training while they live at home with you. And the way you communicate spiritual truth to your children is not by pulling out the old family Bible and dusting it off once a week to have a forced devotional with your children. It's fine to have a devotional time, but spiritual instruction ought to be a part of everyday life. It ought to happen when you sit at the dinner table or when you're in your car in the drive-through. Use that time to talk to your children about spiritual truth. When you're watching a television program and observe something that goes against God's truth, use that as a teaching opportunity. Look for teachable moments to communicate spiritual truth.

Parents, if you're trying to raise godly children in this godless culture, you are swimming upstream. Every day your children are being assaulted through the media, through friends, and through life experiences with values that are contrary to God's values. That's why we have to be proactive in teaching spiritual truth to our children.[3]

I am deeply grateful for the dedicated Christian men and women who faithfully serve our nation's children as educators and administrators. My own mother, a devoted Christian, taught for many years in a public school. But the sad truth is that many of America's primary and secondary schoolteachers do not believe in God or value His Word. And if your children go to college, they will likely encounter worldviews that are foolish or just plain evil. Before they pursue education at a university, your children must have a solid foundation in God's Word and in logic.

In many of today's institutions of higher learning, Christian and conservative opinions are mocked or are forbidden outright. And many of today's scholars fit the description made by the apostle Paul in Romans 1:22: "Professing to be wise, they became fools." And millions of students are paying through the nose to participate in this indoctrination. Government-backed loans encourage students to amass debt and continue to inflate the cost of college—year after year—far beyond what it should be.

If you have children, I urge you to love them, discipline them, and instill in them godly values as well as a deep knowledge of God's Word. Encourage them to memorize Scripture. It will reap lifelong rewards. And above all, share the gospel of Jesus Christ with them.

If you are a teacher, thank you for your hard work and willingness to serve the Lord in our education system. You have an opportunity to influence the next generation greatly. Many of the students coming through your classroom do not have a godly foundation at home. While you cannot be a parent to them, ask God to show you how you can positively influence them and plant seeds of truth that will blossom in their lives later.

If you are a high school or college student, then you are in an exciting time of learning and of maturing into a successful adult. If you have godly parents, remember what they taught you. If you don't, then take it upon yourself to learn and memorize God's Word for yourself. Get involved in a Bible-believing church, and make friends with fellow Christians. Do your best in school as an act of worship to God. Respect your teachers, but realize that some of them may not be friendly to godly values or God's truth. Use the time to develop your own critical thinking. Take in the good; discard the bad.

And all of us need to pray that parents in America take seriously the responsibility of training their children in wisdom and godliness. Pray for reform in American universities. Educating our nation's children is work, but it will yield lasting rewards and will help ensure a lasting legacy for future generations.

⋆ ⋆ ⋆   A Prayer for America   ⋆ ⋆ ⋆

Heavenly Father, You are the perfect Parent who teaches us. Help us to train our nation's children well. You created our brains, and You created us to learn. Help us lead our children in the way that they should go. Give us patience and persistence. Help us to train them according to their own unique bent. Show us how to reform America's broken education system. Fill us with Your Spirit and with a hunger for learning. May we do this all for Your glory, Lord Jesus. In Your name we pray. Amen.

⋆ ⋆ ⋆

The fear of the Lord is the beginning of knowledge,
but fools despise wisdom and instruction.

—Proverbs 1:7 niv

16

For Pure Sexuality

In 1752, a large bell arrived in Philadelphia from England. The Pennsylvania Colony had purchased it for their statehouse (later known as Independence Hall). On the bell were inscribed the words of Leviticus 25:10 (KJV): "Proclaim liberty throughout all the land unto all the inhabitants thereof." This verse refers to the Old Testament year of jubilee, which occurred every fifty years. During the year of jubilee, the Israelites were to cancel debts and free their slaves.

However, because the metal used to forge the bell was brittle, it cracked during its very first strike. So, the bell was melted down and recast. More metals were added to strengthen it, as well as to make it ring more sweetly. But it still bore the jubilant words of Scripture. Once refinished, it was named the State House Bell and was used to gather lawmakers to meetings and the townsfolk for the news.

On July 8, 1776, the bell was rung to celebrate the first public reading of the Declaration of Independence. It literally rang in freedom for the nation! When the British invaded Philadelphia a few years later, the large bell was hidden in a church until it could be safely returned to the statehouse.

In 1835, an abolitionist group adopted the bell with its inspirational quote as their symbol. They dubbed it the Liberty Bell and hoped it would serve as a powerful impetus to free literal slaves. Since then, women's suffrage groups and civil rights advocates have used the Liberty Bell as a reminder of the freedom promised to all Americans in the Declaration of Independence.

No one is sure exactly when the bell began to crack again. But by 1846, a large breach was visible. Attempts were made that year to repair the bell for a celebration of George Washington's birthday on February 22. According to reports, it started ringing loudly and clearly that cold morning. But by evening, it was fractured beyond repair, rendered unusable, and taken out of commission.

In the late 1800s, the bell traveled around the country for displays at expositions and fairs. To a nation healing from the Civil War, the Liberty Bell served as a cogent reminder of a time when the nation fought together, united for a noble cause. It finally came to rest back in Philadelphia as a symbol of America's independence and liberty. To this day, millions of people visit the Liberty Bell each year.

When discussing America's current ideas of liberty—especially sexual liberty—it is hard to imagine a more apt analogy than the Liberty Bell.

Just like the Liberty Bell, America's ideas of freedom came from England and were firmly rooted in Scripture. However, they needed to be recast on this continent, with more influences added. This gave the concept strength and beauty. The ideals of liberty—based in the Bible—rang in our independence. During times of struggle, it was kept safe in our churches. And over the decades, that clarion call of freedom was sent throughout the land, mustering those who had been denied their rights to take their place—a place guaranteed in the Declaration of Independence—in the land of the free.

But somewhere along the way, the idea became cracked. Instead of meaning freedom from tyranny to worship God as our conscience dictated, in modern America, "freedom" has come to mean "licentiousness." People today want "freedom" not from tyranny but from God's commands, including His design for sex and sexuality. This is a "freedom" that leads to bondage.

Since the beginning of time Satan has been dangling a lie in front of us that says, "Sin leads to freedom." Isn't that the line he used on Eve in the garden? He said, "Eve, the reason God doesn't want you to eat of this tree is because He doesn't want you to experience the exhilaration, the happiness you deserve. If you will disobey God in this area, you can have true freedom." But sin never leads to freedom; it always leads to slavery. The fact is, you cannot sin just a little bit and stop. When you sin once, you sin again and again. Peter said it this way in 2 Peter 2:19: "By what a man is overcome, by this he is enslaved." Some of you right now are engaged in pornography, premarital sex, or an adulterous relationship, and you say, "I can stop any time I want." Really? Then why aren't you stopping now? The fact is, sin never leads to freedom. It always leads to slavery. In Proverbs 5:22, Solomon said, "His own iniquities will capture the wicked, and he will be held with the cords of his own sin."[1]

But following God's rules actually leads to true freedom and happiness. As the apostle Paul wrote in Galatians 5:13, "For you were called to freedom, brethren; only do not turn your freedom into an opportunity for the flesh, but through love serve one another."

Thankfully, our nation's ideas of freedom can be recast. Emblazoned with the Word of God, spiritual liberty can once again ring out across our land, proclaiming true freedom for those formerly enslaved by the tyranny of sin. As Jesus said:

The Spirit of the Lord is upon Me,
Because He anointed Me to preach the gospel to the poor.

He has sent Me to proclaim release to the captives,
And recovery of sight to the blind,
To set free those who are oppressed,
To proclaim the favorable year of the Lord. (Luke 4:18–19)

No matter what you may have done in the past, God promises that He will forgive you and give you a new start. I urge you, repent of your sins and find true freedom in Jesus Christ today.[2]

★ ★ ★ A Prayer for America ★ ★ ★

Heavenly Father, You sent Your beloved Son, Jesus Christ, to die on a cross to cancel my sin debt and to free me from the tyranny of sin and of Satan. You have raised me to spiritual life from death. You call me to leave the tomb of slavery and to be unbound from the rags of sin. How can I be entangled in them again? Help me to run from sexual temptation. Give me accountability partners who will help me walk the path to true freedom. Help me to deny myself, take up my cross, and follow You in love and service to others. Empower me to do this through the Holy Spirit. In Your name I pray, Lord Jesus. Amen.

★ ★ ★

Jesus answered them, "Truly, truly, I say to you,
everyone who commits sin is the slave of sin…
If the Son makes you free, you will be free indeed."

—JOHN 8:34–36

For Godly Marriages

America's history is filled with examples of godly marriages that have made our nation strong. One of my favorite examples is the legacy of Billy and Ruth Graham.

Ruth Bell was born in 1920 to Presbyterian medical missionaries serving in China. As a girl, she trusted in Jesus as her Savior and planned to become a missionary to Tibet—that is, until she met a young man preparing for ministry while at college.

William (Billy) Graham was born in 1918 in North Carolina. When he was sixteen, Billy trusted Jesus as his Savior. After graduating high school, he attended the Florida Bible Institute. There, Billy felt called by God to become an evangelist. He then went to Wheaton College to prepare for ministry.

When Billy first met Ruth at Wheaton, he was interested in her but also intimidated because she was pretty and popular. He finally worked up the courage to ask her out, and she said yes.

For their first date, Billy took Ruth to a performance of Handel's *Messiah*. Afterward, walking her back to her apartment, Billy tried to hold Ruth's hand, but she pulled away. *Well, I've failed with this one*, Billy thought, and he left, dejected. But Ruth was more interested than she let on. "Lord, if You'd let me serve You with that man, I'd consider it the greatest privilege of my life," she prayed that night.

"It's a good thing I didn't know what lay ahead," she later admitted, with a smile. "Otherwise I wouldn't have had the nerve to pray such a prayer."

Billy graduated in 1943. He and Ruth were married a few months later.

In 1948, Billy became world-famous during an evangelistic crusade he led in Los Angeles. From then on, he frequently traveled, often for weeks or months at a time. While Billy was away, Ruth had to raise their five children at home alone. It was tough, but, like everything else, she gave it to God. "Any other wife in the world…would have said, 'I can't believe you're leaving me again,'" their daughter Anne recalled. "But I never heard Mother complain."

"In our home, my wife has had to be father and mother. And she has done a magnificent job," Billy said.

"For me, it would have been very difficult to have him gone so much of the time for any other reason than that of sharing Jesus Christ with other people," Ruth said.

Ruth was an avid student of the Bible and an author. She helped Billy with sermon illustrations and editing. "I have never prepared a sermon without consulting her on it first," Billy once told a reporter.

Their son Ned observed, "There never would have been a Billy Graham, without a Ruth Graham."

Billy and Ruth were married for sixty-three years. "We wouldn't have lasted this long without the Lord and his presence," Ruth once said. "He [Jesus] was the Lord of both of our lives. And like the spokes of a wheel, the closer you get to the center—to God—the closer you get to one another."

"Every marriage has its difficulties," Billy said. "True love comes from God."[1]

Marriage between one man and one woman was the first human institution God ever created. In Genesis 1:26–2:25, God established and blessed marriage as the building block of all civilization. Study after study proves that when the family begins to break down, so does the culture. We are seeing some of the consequences of that right now in our nation. As the family goes, so goes the nation.

God meant marriage to be a picture of Christ's love for His bride, the church. Even though both spouses are equal, God has given different roles and responsibilities to husbands and wives if the home is to function properly.[2] In Ephesians 5:22–33, the apostle Paul explained that a husband's role is to love his wife, lead his family, and be himself subject to Jesus Christ. A wife is to love God and be subject to the Christlike leadership of her husband. When both spouses are committed to serving the Lord and each other in this way, then they fulfill God's design for a faithful, loving marriage.

When asked for his advice about marriage, Billy offered the following words of wisdom:

A strong marriage actually needs to include three people: the husband, the wife—and God. Begin your life together, therefore, by committing your lives and your marriage to Jesus Christ. Remember: marriage isn't just a social convenience or a legal custom. Marriage comes from God, and it is one of His greatest gifts to us. When times of stress or disappointment come (and they will), remember that God brought you together, and you made your marriage vows not only to each other but also to Him. Never forget Jesus' words: 'Therefore what God has joined together, let no one separate' (Mark 10:9 [NIV])."[3]

You may not be called to preach the gospel to millions of people around the world like Billy Graham. But you are called to serve Jesus, wherever you are. And if you are married, then you are called to love and respect your mate as you love and respect God. Whenever you are tempted to be selfish or unloving, ask God to help you place your mate's interests above your own, as Paul commanded in Philippians 2:3–4: "Do nothing from selfishness or empty conceit, but with humility of mind regard one another as more important than yourselves; do not merely look out for your own personal interests, but also for the interests of others."[4]

And regardless of your marital status, we should all ask God to strengthen marriages throughout America. Godly homes will sustain the success of our nation.

★ ★ ★ A Prayer for America ★ ★ ★

Heavenly Father, strong marriages are the foundation of a healthy society. You invented marriage to be a picture of the love that You, Your Son, and Your Spirit have shared for all eternity. Teach husbands to love their wives as Christ loves His bride, the church, and teach wives to be subject to their husbands as the church is to Jesus Christ. Teach us to work through our problems and to love each other as we should. Please strengthen marriages in America, and may we make You, Lord Jesus, the center of our homes. Protect us all from the evil one. In Jesus' name I pray. Amen.

★ ★ ★

Wives, be subject to your husbands,
as is fitting in the Lord. Husbands, love your wives
and do not be embittered against them.

—Colossians 3:18–19

For the Voiceless

In 1976, a seventeen-year-old girl slept with her boyfriend and conceived a child. She didn't want to be a teenage mother, so seven and a half months into her pregnancy, she walked into a Planned Parenthood clinic to find a solution.

"The fetus is not a person," the staff reassured her, "but an unfeeling clump of cells." The young lady breathed a sigh of relief. With her permission, the abortionist injected a saline solution directly into the mother's womb. Normally, the unborn child gulps the solution, which burns the baby—inside and out—causing excruciating death, usually within twenty-four hours.

But this time, despite her mother's and the abortionist's best efforts, after eighteen hours of suffering, a 2.75-pound living baby girl entered the world at just twenty-nine weeks' gestation.

Her mother named her Gianna.

"I was born at the perfect moment," Gianna recounts. "The abortionist wasn't at work yet. Had he been there, he would have strangled me, suffocated me, or thrown me into a trashcan. But a nurse was able to call an ambulance [and] had me transferred to a hospital, thereby saving my life."[1]

Miraculously, Gianna not only lived, but she suffered no burns, blindness, or damage to her vocal cords from the saline solution. The attempt on Gianna's life, however, did take a toll on her tiny frame.

"You experienced the highest level of physical and emotional trauma that you possibly could," a doctor later told Gianna. Physically, the trauma of the abortion resulted in a lack of oxygen to her brain, causing Gianna to develop cerebral palsy (CP)—an incurable, lifelong movement disorder.

Once Gianna gained enough strength, she was placed into emergency foster care and eventually ended up in the loving arms of a woman named Penny.

"Because of her CP, Gianna will never be anything more than a vegetable the rest of her life," the doctors told Penny.

"Penny just ignored all of that," Gianna said. "And thank God. She prayed for me and she did my physical therapy three times a day. I began to hold up my head, sit up, crawl, and walk by the age of three and a half with a walker and leg braces."

Despite Gianna's progress under Penny's care, no family wanted to adopt a child with CP—until Penny's own daughter did so, making Penny Gianna's grandmother.

Penny lived the love of Christ, so when Gianna heard the gospel from her mother at the tender age of three or four, Gianna pushed aside her walker, took off her leg braces, got on her knees, and trusted Jesus as her Savior. *He's the one who is going to help me*, she thought.

And He did. "Now I walk without a walker and without leg braces," Gianna declared. And she added, "I have also run two marathons!" Penny got to see all of that before she passed away in 2014. "She was my heart," Gianna said. "She and Jesus are the reason I am me."

Since 1973, when the Supreme Court denied the personhood of every unborn child in the landmark *Roe v. Wade* decision, Americans have murdered more than 61.2 million babies through abortion.[2] Every day in the United States, we murder three thousand innocent babies in the womb.[3] Thousands more are killed through oral contraceptives.[4]

When we look at history, we can see how God deals with nations that murder children. God raised up the Babylonians and Assyrians to invade Israel for practicing child sacrifice. God used the Allied Forces to crush Nazi Germany for sending trainloads of children to gas chambers. Do we really have to wonder about God's attitude toward a nation like ours that sanctions the killing of millions of children?[5]

We cannot plead ignorance. Modern science confirms the personhood of every child from the moment of conception. The child in the womb has DNA unique from that of the mother, and by as early as six weeks, the baby's heartbeat can be detected.[6] By eight weeks, the baby has its own unique fingerprints;[7] and by twenty weeks, the baby in the womb can feel pain.[8] The more we know, the more culpable we become.

God has given America more than forty-five years to correct this great evil. But God's patience will not last forever. The blood of millions of unborn children cries out to Him. Who will be the voice for these defenseless infants?

As Christians, you and I are called to be "ambassadors for Christ" (2 Cor. 5:20). We must articulate God's views to those within God's kingdom and to those living outside of it. We must vote for courageous pro-life candidates and support causes that protect the unborn. We must also show the love of Christ to women who are contemplating abortion and help them in practical ways. "Be with the woman in crisis," Gianna advised. "Listen to her. Make sure her needs are met. Then take her to a local pregnancy resource center. Their services are free."

With God's help, we can work together to end the abomination that is abortion. God expects nothing less from us.

★ ★ ★   **A Prayer for America**   ★ ★ ★

Lord Jesus, Your heart weeps for the millions of unborn babies mur-dered in our country every year. You have been patient with us, giving us decades to repent. Heavenly Father, change the hearts of Americans to see abortion for the evil that it is. Give courage and urgency to our lawmakers to protect Your innocent image bearers. Touch the hearts of mothers who are considering aborting their babies, and help them see that every child is a gift from You. If they are unable or unwilling to take care of their babies, then show them that adoption is the loving option. Show me ways I can care for and support these mothers during their pregnancies, and make clear if You want me to adopt a child. Raise up Christians across our nation who are also willing to help these mothers and care for their children. Bring those who have participated in abortion to repentance, and let them know that You offer mercy, forgiveness, and healing through Your Son, Jesus Christ. In His name we pray, amen.

★ ★ ★

For you created my inmost being;
you knit me together in my mother's womb.
—Psalm 139:13 NIV

19

For the Crisis of Fatherless Children

Edward Flanagan was born in Ireland on July 13, 1886, the eighth of eleven children. His family was poor, and Edward frequently fell ill. But he had an advantage that many young men do not have: a devoted father and a nurturing mother. "The old-fashioned home with fireside companionship, its religious devotion and its closely-knit family ties is my idea of what a home should be. My Father would tell me many stories that were interesting to a child…It was from him I learned the great science of life and heard examples from the lives of saints, scholars and patriots," he said.[1]

Flanagan felt called to ministry at an early age, so in 1904, he immigrated to America to attend college and then seminary. In 1912, he was ordained as a Catholic priest and served at his first parish in O'Neill, Nebraska, and then in Omaha.

In the harsh Nebraska winter of 1915–16, Flanagan set up a shelter that housed men who were out of work due to a drought. When the United States joined World War I in April 1917, most of the able-bodied men in the shelter enlisted. Flanagan's shelter then filled with jailbirds and drifters from all over who could not hold a job. As he talked to them, he soon realized that their stories were almost always the same: None came from intact, loving families. All were victims of parental neglect, desertion, divorce, or death.[2]

So Flanagan began working with boys in the juvenile court system, and in 1917, he opened Father Flanagan's Boys' Home in downtown Omaha. His home quickly outgrew several buildings, and in 1921, Father Flanagan moved to Overlook Farm, ten miles west of Omaha. Flanagan went to great lengths to find and bring in the neediest and most helpless boys—even boys who had been in prison for serious crimes. He knew they needed a father figure who would love them, protect them, show Christ to them, and train them for life. He accepted "all boys, regardless of race, creed, or cultural background,"[3] which was unusual for the time.

Flanagan became a father to these boys, and he taught them responsibility and a trade. His boys went to school, chapel, and the gymnasium. They elected a "boy mayor" as well as voted for other posts and policies. In fact, in 1926, the boys voted to change the title of Overlook Farm to Boys Town. Flanagan encouraged each boy to pray to God but did not tell them what denomination to be. He tried to exemplify a faithful life to them, faithfully praying in the chapel every morning before dawn.

Even through the tough years of the Great Depression, Boys Town grew. In 1934, they created their own fire station and post office, and in 1936, Boys Town became an official village in the state of Nebraska.

In 1939, MGM studios released the movie *Boys Town*. Spencer Tracy won an Academy Award for his portrayal of Father Flanagan, and the Academy of Motion Pictures Arts and Sciences gave a special Oscar to Father Flanagan for his work.

During World War II, as many as one thousand former citizens of Flanagan's Boys Town served in the US military. Hundreds of them listed Flanagan as their next of kin. Because of this, the American War Dads Association declared him "America's #1 War Dad." Flanagan displayed this title proudly, and he did what he could for his boys. He crisscrossed the country raising money for the effort by selling war bonds. He traveled to military posts overseas to raise morale, and he assisted the attorney general to measure the effects of the war on families.

After the war, Father Flanagan traveled to thirty-one states and twelve countries in Europe and Asia, helping to establish homes for at-risk youth. He died in Germany on May 15, 1948, during one of these trips. At his death, he was honored by president Harry S. Truman.

Today, Boys Town has facilities in ten states, Washington, DC, and many other nations. In fact, eighty-nine programs around the world have been established and modeled after Flanagan's example. The Boys Town organization also runs two hospitals, a national training center, and a national hotline. Each year, Boys Town cares for 1.4 million youth and families in the United States.[4] That's the difference one father figure can make!

We desperately need father figures in America. Today, as many as 25 percent of American children live in homes without fathers.[5] David Popenoe has written about the effects of children in fatherless homes. Seventy percent of long-term prison inmates, 60 percent of rapists, and 72 percent of adolescent murderers grew up in fatherless homes.[6] Additionally, almost all mass shooters come from fatherless homes.[7]

Most single mothers do the best they can for their children. And not all fatherless homes can be avoided. But God designed children to be raised in a home with both a mother and a father. The sexual revolution, no-fault divorce, redefining marriage, and our welfare state contribute to the fatherless epidemic. But so has a personal abandonment of God and His Word. We must return to biblical principles and a relationship with our heavenly Father through His Son, Jesus Christ.

Christian men, I encourage you to look for ways to be father figures to the fatherless children in your church and community, whether it's through coaching sports, volunteering at church, or reaching out to single mothers and widows to spend time with their children on a consistent basis. And fathers, God's Word says you need to accept both the responsibility and the blessings you have been given of leading your family and of raising your children to know the Lord.

If you are a father and have not been there for your children, you can find amazing grace by trusting in Jesus Christ as the payment of your sins, including the sin of abandonment. In Him, you will find forgiveness and healing as well as the possibility of restoration. And if you don't know how to be a father, you have the perfect Father in heaven. He will train you if you ask Him. Seek out godly men at your church and their guidance in being the father God wants you to be.

The same goes if you had an absent father. Look at the psalmist's words, written for you: "My father and my mother have forsaken me, but the LORD will take me up" (Ps. 27:10). Your heavenly Father is glad to call you His child. In fact, He loves you so much that He sent His only Son, Jesus Christ, to die on a cross for your sins and rise from the dead so that He could adopt you into His everlasting family. And Jesus gladly went through with it, saving you so that He could be your older brother, as well as your God and King.

★ ★ ★ A Prayer for America ★ ★ ★

Heavenly Father, thank You being my perfect Father. Throughout our nation, turn the hearts of fathers to their children and children to their fathers. Remind fathers what a blessing and responsibility it is to raise their children. Help mothers to seek godly men to be fathers or father figures for their children. And help Christian men all across our country to step up to serve as father figures for a generation of fatherless children. Teach our nation's men how to be good fathers and husbands again. Thank You for the good and heroic fathers we do have. In Jesus' name I pray. Amen.

* * *

A father of the fatherless and a judge for the widows,
Is God in His holy habitation.

—PSALM 68:5

For Those in Prison

Jack Murphy was born in Los Angeles in 1938. His parents moved around a lot, working on different military bases. Jack was a smart, driven kid, and he learned to play tennis and the violin. On base, he saw American troops doing meaningful work. But no one mentored young Jack to know the Lord or to be a godly man.

Jack eventually ended up at the University of Pittsburgh. But, as he put it, "I got tired of the snow."[1] So he hitchhiked to Miami in 1955 when he was eighteen. He lived it up in South Florida, womanizing, smoking marijuana, and crashing celebrity parties. He made money teaching tennis, swimming lessons, hustling at pool, selling straw hats, and building surfboards. During one tropical storm, Jack stayed out in the ocean, expertly riding monster waves. In this way he earned the nickname "Murph the Surf." He was later inducted into the surfing hall of fame.

Murph's hedonistic lifestyle took a toll on his relationships. One girlfriend committed suicide, and two marriages fell apart. After his second divorce in 1963, one of his businesses also failed. Distraught and broke, Murph fell in with other aimless people who began robbing South Florida mansions. Murph's cut from his first jewel heist was $15,000 ($124,000 in today's money). Murph was hooked. He joined their gang and soon began breaking into more estates.

Murph and his gang started working jobs all over America and beyond. Then they found the American Museum of Natural History in New York City. It housed the world's most precious gem collection, including the golf-ball–sized Star of India sapphire. Not including the Star, the precious-stone collection was insured for more than $400,000 ($3.25 million in today's money). Security was lax, so on October 29, 1964, using grappling hooks and rope, Murph's gang climbed to the fourth story, crept along a ledge, and entered through an open window. They stole the jewels and escaped the same way.

Two days later, Murph and his accomplices were arrested. They were convicted, and each received three-year sentences, of which they served two. Many newspapers hailed the heist as the crime of the century, and in 1975, a movie was made about their actions, glamorizing the thieves.

But Murph's life was far from glamorous after prison. He had developed a cocaine habit and returned to theft to support his addiction. During one robbery, he pistol-whipped an elderly woman. After another job, he killed a fellow thief who threatened to talk if she didn't get a bigger share. In 1969, Murph received two life sentences, plus twenty years, for the murder and beating.

Of course, "life" in prison rarely means that, and Murph would be eligible for parole in 2005. But Murph had slid far into darkness. "I ran a drug ring. I ran a gambling operation. I was out of control. I helped lead a prison strike in 1971 and ended up in isolation for seven months, on death row," he recalled.[2]

In the early 1970s, the prison warden opened Florida's jails to counselors, educators, job trainers, and missionaries. Soon Christians began writing and coming to the prisons to mentor inmates and to share how Jesus had saved them.

This went on for years. Eventually, in 1974, the seeds of love and truth that these Christians sowed into Murph's life took root. Jack trusted in Jesus as his Savior. He then joined Alcoholics Anonymous, gave up drugs, and took up painting.

As Murph began growing in Christ, God softened his heart, and waves of remorse began sweeping over him. So he turned to God's Word for comfort. One of his favorite Bible verses was Romans 10:13, which says, "Whoever will call on the name of the Lord will be saved." As he accepted Christ's forgiveness, Murph learned to forgive all the others who had hurt him. He became free long before he ever got out of jail.

Murph learned to use his time in prison wisely. He joined the prison chaplaincy program. He led Bible studies and taught prisoners to read and write. He even began mediating disputes between convicts and prison guards. Eventually, the warden took notice and moved Murph's parole date up to November 1986, even advocating for him. Miraculously, the board released Murph early.

As soon as Murph got out, he joined several prison ministries and began visiting correction facilities all across America. He has now visited more than fifteen hundred prisons all over the world. He married a godly woman and has stayed married for three decades. "A man can come out of prison after thirty years, and if they're not saved, seven out of ten go back to prison," he said. "There is no solution except Jesus Christ."[3]

The Bible says, "Remember the prisoners, as though in prison with them" (Heb. 13:3). As anyone who has been involved in prison ministry will tell you, prisons are fertile soil for the gospel. So pray for those in prison, asking God for their salvation and growth in Christ. Pray that they use the remainder of their prison sentence wisely and with integrity. Pray also for their spouses and children at home. There are 2.7 million children in America who have a parent in prison. Children with an incarcerated parent tend to struggle in school and have behavioral problems, and they are more likely to go to prison themselves.[4] They need to know that their loving heavenly Father is there for them.

Pray also for prisoners who reenter society. Many have difficulty finding a job, and two out of three are rearrested.[5] Ask God to prepare released prisoners to be productive members of society and to avoid old habits. This yields more than just personal benefits for the ex-convict. America is stronger when we find ways to integrate reformed prisoners back into normal life. Ask God to prepare a place for them to work and serve once they are released. And prayerfully consider taking a mission trip to a prison or serving in a prison ministry yourself. It will give you a new perspective, and Jesus promises to go with you.

★ ★ ★ A Prayer for America ★ ★ ★

Heavenly Father, I lift up those behind bars. I know that but for Your amazing grace, there go I. For the men and women in prison who had absent fathers, be their heavenly Father. Even if they came from a good background and simply made terrible decisions, show them that Your grace is for them. Surround inmates with godly influences. Bring hope and truth to them through the gospel. Give them training and mentoring to be productive, faithful members of society. Show me if You want me to be involved with prison ministry, for as Matthew 9:37 says, "The harvest is plentiful, but the workers are few." Lord, send out workers into Your harvest. In Jesus' name I pray. Amen.

★ ★ ★

Lift up your eyes and look on the fields,
that they are white for harvest.

—JOHN 4:35

21

For the Hurting

It's easy to praise God when life is going well. But what do we do when we are hit with sorrow after sorrow? The story of Horatio and Anna Spafford gives us some insight.

Horatio Gates Spafford Jr. was born on October 20, 1828, to a wealthy and well-connected family in New York. He received a good education and decided to become a lawyer. In 1856, he relocated to Chicago. There, Spafford became a senior partner in a large and successful law firm. He then invested his money in real estate in downtown Chicago and became quite wealthy himself.

Spafford taught Sunday school and served as an elder in his Presbyterian church. He loved the Lord and longed to see lost people saved. He worked to abolish slavery, visited inmates in prison, and supported several evangelists, including his good friend Dwight L. Moody.

One day, the dynamic, successful, hard-driving Spafford met a pretty Norwegian immigrant named Anna in his Sunday school class. In September 1861, they married and soon moved into a luxurious estate named Lake View. It came complete with twelve acres and a host of servants. By 1871, the Spaffords had four beautiful daughters. In the spring of that year, Horatio made another promising real-estate investment. Life was good for the Spaffords, and they served God faithfully.

But that was all about to change. In October of that year, the Great Fire of Chicago tore through the city and destroyed most of Spafford's real-estate investments, burning up his fortune in a billow of smoke. But instead of despairing, Spafford and his family began helping the multitudes in the city who were now homeless. This they continued for almost two years as Chicago rebuilt. But then, Spafford's fortunes took another hit in September, with the financial panic of 1873.

After two years of such stress, a doctor recommended a change of scenery for the Spaffords. Horatio and Anna decided to take the family on a trip to England to help evangelist Dwight L. Moody, who planned to lead a revival there. Afterward, the Spaffords would vacation with friends in Europe.

The Spaffords traveled by train to New York in November and were all set to cross the Atlantic when Horatio received word of another business emergency. While he dealt with the problem, he sent Anna and their four daughters ahead on the luxurious French ship *Ville du Havre* on November 15. He planned to follow a few days later.

But by November 22, he still was not able to leave. That same night, in the middle of the icy Atlantic, the *Ville du Havre* collided with another vessel and sank. Of the 313 passengers onboard, 226 drowned.

For over a week, Spafford knew the ship had sunk, but he had no idea what had become of his family. Then, on December 1, a telegram was delivered to his office. It was from Anna!

"Saved alone. What shall I do,"[1] it began.

Spafford collapsed in his chair. All four of their daughters—aged three to eleven—had died. Anna alone survived and was staying with a minister friend in Paris.

Horatio left for France the next day. Four days into his journey across the ocean, the captain notified Spafford that they were over the exact point where the *Ville du Havre* had gone down. According to another daughter, born to the Spaffords after the tragedy, when they reached that point, Horatio returned to his cabin and penned the poem "It Is Well with My Soul." It begins:

When peace, like a river, attendeth my way,
When sorrows, like sea billows roll;
Whatever my lot, Thou hast taught me to say,
It is well, it is well with my soul.

How could Horatio say his soul was doing well? He told us in the next verse:

Though Satan should buffet, though trials should come,
Let this blessed assurance control,
That Christ has regarded my helpless estate,
And hath shed His own blood for my soul.

Horatio and Anna knew that God loved them and was in control. He proved His love by sending His own Son to die on a cross for their sins. The Spafford children died when they were very young or after they had trusted in Jesus as their Savior. Horatio and Anna knew that all of them were in the loving arms of Jesus. They would one day see their darlings again in paradise. As Horatio wrote to his sister-in-law a week later, "On Thursday last we passed over the spot where she went down, in mid-ocean, the waters three miles deep. But I do not think of our dear ones there. They are safe, folded, the dear lambs."[2]

But in the present, it hurt terribly. Eventually, the Spaffords learned to trust God's perfect timing. As Anna told a pastor after the wreck, "God gave me four daughters. Now they have been taken from me. Someday I will understand why."[3]

The Spaffords made it through these tragedies because they were firmly rooted in God's Word, and they trusted Him. They also had Christian friends who upheld them and walked alongside them through the sorrow.

Many people in America today are not a part of a local church. As a result, they are sitting prey when Satan attacks. And make no mistake: Satan will attack. God has called you to be a part of His family, the church, to uphold you.

If you are not already part of a local church, pray that God will lead you to a congregation where Christians "love one another" as Christ has loved us (John 13:34). Ask God to help you connect with fellow believers who "bear one another's burdens" (Gal. 6:2) and are "kind to one another, tender-hearted, forgiving each other, just as God in Christ also has forgiven [us]" (Eph. 4:32). As Christians, we need each other.

Likewise, if God has helped you through a tough time, look for others you can help. After they lost their children, Horatio and Anna felt called by God to start a home for orphans and the destitute in Jerusalem. They did this in 1881, and the Spafford Children's Center continues to serve Jerusalem and the West Bank to this day. The apostle Paul said, "Blessed be the God and Father of our Lord Jesus Christ, the Father of mercies and God of all comfort, who comforts us in all our affliction so that we will be able to comfort those who are in any affliction with the comfort with which we ourselves are comforted by God" (2 Cor. 1:3–4).

Three years after Spafford wrote "It Is Well with My Soul," the Christian composer Philip Bliss set the poem to music. It has since become the most widely used hymn of comfort for grieving Christians. Bliss named the tune of this hymn "Ville du Havre," after the ship. *Ville du Havre* means "Harbor Town" in French, but it can also be translated as "City of Refuge."[4] The church is our city of refuge—our safe haven during life's storms—until Jesus returns.

★ ★ ★ A Prayer for America ★ ★ ★

Heavenly Father, You sent Jesus into our painful existence. Your Word describes Him as a man of sorrows, acquainted with grief. Jesus, I know You are able to comfort me, because You experienced my pain and struggles. I look forward to the day when You will wipe away every tear from my eyes, and there will no longer be any death, mourning, crying, or pain. Bring me healing for my sorrows, and help me to share that healing with others. Come quickly, Lord Jesus. In Your name I pray. Amen.

★ ★ ★

Blessed are those who mourn,
for they shall be comforted.

—MATTHEW 5:4

To Know History
and Learn from It

George Santayana once said, "Those who cannot remember the past are condemned to repeat it."[1] Ever since the fall of man, human nature has not changed, Satan's schemes have not changed, and God's character and purposes have not changed. Because of this, similar situations seem to happen over and over in history. As Solomon observed some three thousand years ago, "What has been will be again, what has been done will be done again; there is nothing new under the sun" (Eccles. 1:9 NIV).

But we can learn from history. For this reason, we set up monuments and statues. Throughout the Old Testament, God commanded His people to set up memorials to remember the miraculous ways He intervened for them. For example, when the Israelites miraculously crossed the Jordan River in Joshua 4:4–9, Joshua called twelve men and commanded them to each take a stone from the middle of the river. He explained, "Let this be a sign among you, so that when your children ask later, saying, 'What do these stones mean to you?' then you shall say to them, 'Because the waters of the Jordan were cut off before the ark of the covenant of the LORD; when it crossed the Jordan, the waters of the Jordan were cut off.' So these stones shall become a memorial to the sons of Israel forever" (Josh. 4:6–7). Creating memorials like this to remember how God has helped us in the past bolsters our faith and brings glory to God.

We also establish monuments to remember either the heroism or the foolishness of our forebears. We honor significant people of the past, but we neither idolize nor demonize them. And we certainly don't forget them. Rather, we take a long, honest look. This motivates us to right action for the future.

This is what Texas general Samuel Houston wanted to do in April 1836. With Mexico's approval, many Americans had settled in the Mexican-controlled area of Texas in the 1820s under the leadership of Stephen F. Austin. The region was far removed from Mexico City, so the inhabitants of Texas enjoyed much autonomy. However, in 1833, General Antonio López de Santa Anna became president of Mexico. He wanted more control of Texas, so Mexico halted all immigration from the United States and enacted heavy duties on goods imported from the United States into Texas.

But most of all, he wanted to remove the guns. Mexican troops marched on the town of Gonzales, east of San Antonio, on October 2, 1835, and demanded that the residents bring out their cannon and hand it over. The town residents responded with "Come and take it!" A battle ensued, and the Mexican forces were defeated. If Santa Anna had studied his history, he would have realized that the Texans were repeating the battle cry of the American revolutionaries against the British at Fort Morris in 1778. He might have realized the sacrificial resolve of those who wanted freedom, even against a vastly superior army.

But he either did not know or did not care. Santa Anna believed he could subjugate Texas. In response, the Texans organized their own military with Sam Houston as their general. In 1835, the Texans took control of the Alamo—an old Spanish mission in present-day San Antonio—and used it as a fort. Santa Anna decided to make an example of the rebels and unexpectedly moved his army of five thousand soldiers into the area.

Those in the Alamo sent word to all of Texas for help in defending the Alamo. However, only thirty-two soldiers arrived from Gonzalez. Among the defenders in the Alamo were legendary frontiersmen William Travis, James Bowie, and Davy Crockett. These soldiers hoped that Sam Houston's forces would arrive soon, so they refused to surrender. In response, Santa Anna promised to leave no survivors. The siege of the Alamo began on February 23, 1836, and lasted two weeks.

True to his word, Santa Anna killed everyone in the Alamo— nearly 190 people—except for a few women, children, and slaves. He left them alive to tell Texans of his victory. But the battle greatly weakened Santa Anna's army, infuriated many Texans, and gave General Sam Houston time to regroup.

On March 27, Mexican troops captured Texas forces near Goliad, due to the incompetence of Texas colonel James Fannin. Then, despite being offered safety by the Mexican commander, Santa Anna ordered all 342 Texas troops killed, including the wounded. Word of Santa Anna's cruelty spread across Texas and united the formerly bickering settlers.

All of this led to April 21. On that day, as Sam Houston prepared his men to face a vastly superior force at San Jacinto, he gave them an impassioned speech and ended with the battle cry, "Remember the Alamo!" Motivated by this remembrance, they routed Santa Anna's forces and gained Texas independence.[2]

Today, the Alamo stands as a reminder of the sacrifice made against tyranny and for liberty. The Texans were not perfect, and the Mexican soldiers were not evil. But the two groups represented two different philosophies of government at the time. We can be thankful that the forces of freedom won the day, and we can learn much by remembering the Alamo.

For any civilization to survive, elders must teach their history to the next generation. We must ensure that our nation's children and grandchildren learn their history. Let's pray that we do not forget our past. Instead, pray that we know it, honor it, and learn from it. Otherwise, those ignorant of the past will become easy prey for Satan's schemes.

★ ★ ★ A Prayer for America ★ ★ ★

Heavenly Father, may we know our history and learn from it. Our fore-fathers often humbly cried out to You in times of trouble, and You heard them. Other times, they acted foolishly, and our nation suffered. Help us learn from the great men and women of our past. May we honor them without idolizing them. Show us how to emulate their strengths and run from their weaknesses. May we always remember Your acts of grace and mercy done on our behalf. Most of all, help us to always remember what You accomplished for us, Lord Jesus, when You died on a cross for us, earning for us everlasting life. And may we never forget how You rose from the dead on the third day and then ascended to heaven. In Your name I pray. Amen.

★ ★ ★

Remember the days of old,
Consider the years of all generations.
Ask your father, and he will inform you,
Your elders, and they will tell you.
—DEUTERONOMY 32:7

23

For Fellow Christians Who Are "Completely Wrong"

Kirsten Powers is a liberal Democrat and a popular political analyst who writes for *USA Today* and often appears on air at CNN. Kirsten and I are on opposite sides on many issues—except the most important one: the preeminence of Jesus Christ. In an article she wrote for *Christianity Today*, Powers described her journey of faith: "If there was one thing in which I was completely secure, it was that I would never adhere to any religion—especially to evangelical Christianity, which I held in particular contempt." But one day, she went to hear pastor Tim Keller preach. At first, she was resistant to the gospel, but for some reason she kept going. After eight months of listening to Keller faithfully share God's Word, Powers began to entertain the idea that Jesus truly was who He said He was.

"My whole world was imploding," she wrote. "How was I going to tell my family or friends about what had happened? Nobody would understand. I didn't understand. (It says a lot about the family in which I grew up that one of my most pressing concerns was that Christians would try to turn me into a Republican.)"

After attending a Bible study one day, she finally trusted Jesus as her Savior. "The world looked entirely different, like a veil had been lifted off it," she said. "I had not an iota of doubt. I was filled with indescribable joy...The Hound of Heaven had pursued me and caught me—whether I like it or not."[1]

Sadly, some Christians doubt Powers's conversion because of people she still associates with. Believe it or not, the religious "conservatives" of the first century had the same problem with Jesus. The Pharisees—the fundamentalists of that day—lambasted Jesus for associating with "tax collectors and sinners" (Matt. 9:11).

Why was hanging out with tax collectors so terrible back then? In the first century, Jews who collected taxes were considered turncoats because they worked for the Roman Empire. (It would be as if China invaded America, and then the Chinese government hired your next-door neighbor to take your money and wire it to Beijing.) If that weren't bad enough, these first-century Jewish tax collectors often charged more from their countrymen than Roman law required and then pocketed the difference. How sleazy can you be?

That was what many in Christ's day thought. "If Jesus is a righteous Jew who follows the Mosaic Law," the religious leaders wondered, "then how could He befriend such double-crossers and thieves?"

How did Jesus respond to this criticism? Did He worry about His reputation with the Pharisees? Not at all! Instead, He called one of these hated tax collectors to be among His own twelve disciples. In Matthew 9:9, Jesus "saw a man called Matthew, sitting in the tax collector's booth; and He said to him, 'Follow Me!' And he got up and followed [Jesus]." This decision must have infuriated Christ's critics. But Acts 10:34 reminds us, "God is not one to show partiality."

Jesus calls both "our kind" as well as "other kinds" of people. So why do we, like the Pharisees, so often question someone's fitness to follow Jesus? We tend to judge people's faithfulness by their denomination or taste in entertainment—or even by their politics.

However, a person's commitment to Christ is determined by his or her faith in and obedience to Christ—not by intellect, denomination, or politics. We must remember that as Christians, our job is not to uphold the platforms of the Republican Party or Democratic Party. Our job is to uphold the platform of Jesus Christ by sharing the gospel and by promoting biblical values. That is why Jesus left His church on the earth.[2]

Believers from every tongue and tribe—including the tribe of liberals—will populate heaven. So, if in the life to come you and I are going to live with people who are different from us, shouldn't we start trying to get along with them in this life?

We must lay aside our prejudices over debatable issues and view our fellow Christians as God views them—as our brothers and sisters in Christ. When unbelievers in America see how Christians from opposite ends of the political spectrum love one another—despite our differences—then they will be more open to hearing about the Savior whom we love and serve. As Jesus declared, "By this all men will know that you are My disciples, if you have love for one another" (John 13:35).

★ ★ ★ A Prayer for America ★ ★ ★

Lord Jesus, teach me to love as You loved. Help me to value and love fellow Christians with whom I disagree. Help me to extend grace, to give others the benefit of the doubt, and to listen twice as much as I talk. Show me how to disagree without being disagreeable. Help all Christians in our nation to uphold biblical values, regardless of political platform. Teach us to be unified in the essentials of the faith, tolerant in the nonessentials, and loving in everything. May the whole world know that we are Your disciples by how we love one another. In Jesus' name I pray. Amen.

★ ★ ★

By this all men will know that you are My disciples,
if you have love for one another.

—JOHN 13:35

To Seize Opportunities
God Gives Us

Opportunities lay all around us. But oftentimes these opportunities come disguised as problems. No one knew this better than Sarah Breedlove. Sarah was born on December 23, 1867, near Delta, Louisiana. She was one of six children and the first in her family born free after Emancipation. Sarah's mother died in 1874, as did her father the following year, when Sarah was only seven. She then moved with her sister and brother-in-law to Vicksburg, Mississippi. There, little Sarah endured abuse from her brother-in-law. She also had to work, sometimes as a domestic servant, sometimes picking cotton. She couldn't go to school and had only three months of formal education from literacy classes her church had offered.

Wanting to start a new life, Sarah married Moses McWilliams when she was fourteen. When she was seventeen, she gave birth to their daughter, A'Lelia. But in 1887, Moses died, leaving nineteen-year-old Sarah alone with their two-year-old daughter. She and A'Lelia then moved to St. Louis, where several of Sarah's brothers worked as barbers. There, Sarah worked as a laundress, making $1.50 a day. Such a salary was barely enough to send her daughter to the city's public schools, which people had to personally pay for in those days.

Sarah faced many hardships, but she wouldn't let them get her down. She trusted God and joined a community of faith at the St. Paul African Methodist Episcopal Church, where she often sang in the choir. Sarah also attended public night school as often as her busy schedule allowed.

In the 1890s, Sarah developed a scalp infection that caused much of her hair to fall out. But Sarah didn't let this get her down, either. She learned about hair care from her brothers and realized her situation was not unique. Sarah started experimenting with store-bought hair products, as well as home remedies, to resolve her condition.

Soon, she met Annie Malone, an African American woman who had started her own hair-care business, the Poro Company. Sarah became a sales representative for Poro when the World's Fair came to St. Louis in 1904. Sales were poor, so in 1905, when she was thirty-seven, Sarah and her daughter uprooted again, moving to Denver with Annie. In addition to working for Malone, Sarah continued to develop and sell her own products on the side. Malone eventually accused Sarah of stealing her formula, although Malone could never prove it.

In 1906, Sarah married Charles Joseph Walker and became known as Madam C. J. Walker. Her husband was also her business partner, and he helped her market her products. Sarah went door to door, selling her wares and educating black women about hair care. Together, the Walkers also developed a mail-order division. In 1906, her daughter took charge of mail orders, while Sarah and Charles traveled the country, selling their products.

In 1908 they relocated to Pittsburgh, where they opened a beauty parlor and a college to train and license "hair culturists." In

1910, they established a base in Indianapolis and then another in Harlem in 1913. In Indianapolis, Sarah built a factory, a hair salon, a beauty school, and a laboratory for research and development. Many of the people she hired to help manage her growing business were women. This was very unusual for the time.

Eventually, the Walkers' sales force grew to several thousand, and by 1917, they had trained nearly twenty thousand associates. Besides crisscrossing the United States, the Madam C. J. Walker company also expanded into the Caribbean and Central America.

In addition to providing cures for scalp ailments, Sarah wanted to bless people in other ways. She taught many underprivileged women how to budget, grow a business, and become financially independent. She encouraged charitable giving and organized a female cosmetic entrepreneurs' association. This group held their first conference in Philadelphia in the summer of 1917—one of the first national gatherings of female entrepreneurs in America.

Sarah gave to many charitable organizations and was a strong patron of the arts. When she died in 1919, she was the wealthiest African American woman in America. In her will, she directed two-thirds of all future net profits from her company to be given to charity. At a time when the yearly salary of the average American was $750, Walker's estate was valued at $600,000 (about $9 million in today's money). This valuation was after she had given away much of her income every year to charity. If not for her generosity, she would have been one of the first self-made female millionaires in America. But the legacy of her hard work, generous giving, faith, and optimistic attitude makes her a much wealthier person than if she had merely had a net worth of a million dollars.[1]

Sarah experienced almost every disadvantage in life. But she never made excuses. Furthermore, she saw the problem of her scalp condition as an opportunity from God, and she jumped at it. We need to do the same. Every hardship is also an opportunity to trust

God, to learn, and to rise above. As Romans 8:28 says, "We know that God causes all things to work together for good to those who love God, to those who are called according to His purpose." Let's pray that we remember that God is in control. And ask God to help us see problems as opportunities and take every opportunity that God brings our way to grow, to help others, and to further expand His kingdom.

★ ★ ★ **A Prayer for America** ★ ★ ★

Heavenly Father, help me to be thankful and to see every problem as an opportunity from You. Father, You are good, and You give me everything I need for life and godliness. You have also set up fruitful work and good deeds that You want me to perform. Help me to be like my Savior, Jesus Christ, who never rushed but lived every day intentionally for You, in perfect trust. It is in His holy name that I pray. Amen.

★ ★ ★

Be careful how you walk, not as unwise men
but as wise, making the most of your time,
because the days are evil.

—Ephesians 5:15–16

25

To Do Our Jobs
as for Jesus

Did you know that you can perform any legitimate work—any activity that isn't sin—as an act of worship to Jesus? God has gifted different people with different talents and abilities. It's true that some jobs pay better than others, and some positions we hold only for short seasons of life, but they can all glorify God. Jesus worked most of His life as a carpenter, and you can bet that He did His work as unto His Father. Working with such an attitude makes those around us more willing to hear what we have to say about spiritual subjects.

Furthermore, in Luke 16:10, Jesus said, "He who is faithful in a very little thing is faithful also in much." In other words, doing menial tasks with excellence also helps prepare us for positions with more responsibilities and rewards.

No one knew this principle better than George Washington Carver. "When you do the common things in life in an uncommon way, you will command the attention of the world," he once said.

Carver was born as a slave in Missouri in 1864, one year before slavery was abolished. His father died before he was born, and his mother and sister were kidnapped when he was only a few weeks old. Thankfully, Carver and his brother were adopted by their former slave owners, who taught them to read and write. Carver worked in the kitchen and garden, where he discovered that he had a talent for plants.

Several times a week, Carver walked to a school ten miles away to receive an education. About this time, a friend led Carver to Christ, and he began reading his Bible every day, a habit that gave him strength for the rest of his life. When Carver was thirteen, he left home and moved to another town to attend high school. He had to pay his own tuition, so Carver worked in the kitchen of a local hotel, developing recipes and entering them in cooking contests.

After graduation, Carver applied to Highland Presbyterian College. His application was impressive, and he was granted a full scholarship. But when Carver arrived, the dean denied him when he saw Carver was black. Carver was heartbroken, but he trusted God. He worked for the next eight years doing odd jobs, saving money, and looking for another college. Finally, he was accepted to study botany at Iowa State Agricultural School.

At Iowa State, Carver was the first black student to earn a bachelor of science degree, in 1894. His professors were so impressed with his work that they asked him to join their faculty. He did, and he earned a master's degree in 1896. He became the director of the Iowa State Experimental Station, where he made several scientific breakthroughs. He had fame and a good salary. But he gave it up when offered the opportunity by Booker T. Washington at Tuskegee Institute to help educate poor black farmers in Alabama. At Tuskegee, he and his students had to rummage through garbage to find materials to make their own laboratory equipment. They used their makeshift lab to save agriculture in the South. They found new uses for peanuts, sweet potatoes, and soybeans. The farmers could now rotate crops and thus replenish the soil, which had been devastated from decades of exclusive cotton growth.

During World War I, Carver helped Henry Ford develop a peanut-based replacement for rubber. After the war, he continued to develop products from his crops. By 1938—largely due to Carver's influence—peanuts had grown into a $200 million crop annually in the United States, the equivalent of $3.5 billion today!

Carver has been honored many times by the US government and others for his hard work and service to others. He also trusted Jesus as his Savior, so he received a "Well done, good and faithful servant" when he entered heaven as well.[1]

Like Carver, we all need to perform every task as if Jesus was our boss, because ultimately, He is. This is an important principle about success. Success is determined not by our position but by our disposition—our attitude. Unsuccessful people think, *If only I had that position in the company or that place on the organizational chart, then I could really be a success.* But successful people know that success is not the title of your work; it's how you perform your work. You can be intelligent and talented, but if you are not willing to put in the hours with a good attitude, then your success, if you achieve any, will be short-lived. Solomon said in Proverbs 22:29, "Do you see a man skilled in his work? He will stand before kings; he will not stand before obscure men." It is not your position but your disposition that determines whether you are a success.

Perhaps you are studying hard in school, but it seems like nobody notices. Other people get scholarships, but not you. Or maybe you are working for a company—you do your job with honesty and diligence, but other people keep getting promoted. God's Word says that we all do our work for God alone. It shouldn't matter whether you are recognized by anyone; Jesus is the one you serve. But the fact is, more often than not, if you do your work with diligence and faithfulness, with an attitude that honors God, you will rise to the top.[2] This is the kind of attitude that keeps not only our economy—and our nation—strong, but also ensures that our work will have an eternal impact.

If you have been lazy or dishonest in your work, I urge you to repent of that today and renew your commitment to work with excellence. And as 1 Peter 3:15 encourages us, be prepared to answer when people ask you about your motivation. Ask for God's help, and pray that all Christians in our nation—regardless of position—do their jobs as for Jesus Christ.

★ ★ ★ A Prayer for America ★ ★ ★

Heavenly Father, help me to be faithful wherever You have placed me. May I do all my work as unto You, Lord Jesus. Your Word says that all labor is beneficial. Help me to work diligently, wisely, and as an act of worship to You. May I perform every task with excellence, knowing that You bless it. Give me patience with a difficult boss or coworkers, knowing that my time with them is temporary and has a perfect purpose. You see everything, and You will reward my honest, hard work. In Jesus' name I pray. Amen.

★ ★ ★

Whatever you do, do your work heartily,
as for the Lord rather than for men, knowing that
from the Lord you will receive the reward of the
inheritance. It is the Lord Christ whom you serve.

—Colossians 3:23–24

For Christians to Produce
Godly Art with Excellence

J. R. was born in Kingsland, Arkansas, on February 26, 1932, the middle of seven children. He grew up poor with a harsh father. But he also grew up in a home infused with Christian faith. When J. R. was twelve, his older brother Jack had a terrible accident with a table saw. Right before he died, Jack said that he saw angels and told his little brother, "Meet me in heaven."

J. R.'s mother taught him to play guitar and piano, and he soaked up the gospel music he heard in church. Although many Christians at the time disapproved, J. R. also learned much from listening to popular music on the radio.

In 1950, he enlisted in the air force, which forced him to choose a name other than "J. R." He chose "John R.," and soon started going by "Johnny." While deployed to Germany, Johnny Cash started his first band, the Landsberg Barbarians.

He was honorably discharged in July 1954, and married his sweetheart, Vivian, a month later. They moved to Memphis, where Cash performed some gospel songs for Sun Records. But he was informed that Sun had just stopped producing gospel music. "Sing me something that you really feel," the producer is rumored to have told him. So he did, and in 1955, Cash recorded two songs with Sun. Cash's songs were successes, and his career took off. In 1958, Johnny Cash left Sun to sign a lucrative contract with Columbia Records. He recorded popular hits as well as a gospel album.

However, Cash also began drinking heavily, taking drugs, and sleeping around. He also had many expensive run-ins with the law. This reckless and sinful behavior ruined his marriage, and in 1966, Vivian filed for divorce and took their four daughters with her.

Cash continued to spiral downward, but his mother and siblings prayed for him. Finally, in 1968, Cash went to a church and rededicated his life to Christ. That same year, he sought the help of friends to get off drugs, and he also remarried.

Although Cash had experienced God's grace, he continued to struggle with addiction for many years. But whenever he stumbled, he repented and turned back to the Lord. Cash was honest about his struggles and his faith in his art. People related to his songs of struggle such as "Cocaine Blues," "Ring of Fire," and "Folsom Prison Blues." But Cash also presented heartfelt calls to repentance and faith in songs such as "The Man Comes Around," "God's Gonna Cut You Down," and "Ain't No Grave."

Cash also made worship and evangelistic material, such as his gospel albums, the movie *Gospel Road: A Story of Jesus*, and his novel about the apostle Paul, *Man in White*.

Cash became good friends with Billy Graham and often performed at Graham's crusades, sharing his testimony. Johnny Cash went home to be with the Lord on September 12, 2003. On his tombstone is written "Meet Me in Heaven."[1]

God invented art. And He invented us to glorify Him in everything, including with art. The apostle Paul said in Ephesians 2:10, "We are His workmanship, created in Christ Jesus for good works, which God prepared beforehand so that we would walk in them."

However, far too often today, "Christian-made" and "excellent" are not considered compatible terms. Some of America's best-made movies and music now have decidedly anti-Christian themes, and some Christian movies and music of recent years are subpar. This should not be. As Colossians 3:23 says, we should work at all things "heartily, as for the Lord rather than for men." In fact, one reason God gave us the Holy Spirit is to empower us to create beautiful art with excellence.

The first instance in the Bible of God filling someone with the Holy Spirit was to make art. In Exodus 31:3–5, God wanted to create beautiful, well-crafted art to adorn the tabernacle, so He chose a man named Bezalel and said, "I have filled him with the Spirit of God in wisdom, in understanding, in knowledge, and in all kinds of craftsmanship, to make artistic designs for work in gold, in silver, and in bronze, and in the cutting of stones for settings, and in the carving of wood, that he may work in all kinds of craftsmanship." Earlier, in Exodus 28:2–3, God endowed other artists with "the spirit of wisdom" to make garments "for glory and for beauty" to be used in worship.

Centuries later, Solomon used another artist, Hiram, who was "filled with wisdom and understanding and skill for doing any work in bronze" to design God's temple (1 Kings 7:14). Much of the Old Testament—which is all inspired by the Holy Spirit—is written in beautiful poetry, prose, and powerful images. Often it discusses unsavory subjects, but it does so honestly and artfully. God clearly wants us to worship Him with excellence, beauty, and truth.

In the New Testament, God has poured out His Spirit—permanently—on all believers.[2] Thus, Christians whom God the Spirit has gifted with artistic talents must develop and use those talents[3] to produce the best art possible.[4] In Philippians 4:8, Paul gave us guidelines for this endeavor: "Whatever is true, whatever is honorable, whatever is right, whatever is pure, whatever is lovely, whatever is of good repute, if there is any excellence and if anything worthy of praise, dwell on these things." Paul certainly had Scripture in mind when he wrote this—but not exclusively. For example, in Acts 17:28, Paul quoted from hymns written by pagan Greek poets about the false god Zeus, and he used their writing to glorify the true God! If pagans can write works worshipping what they do not know, then we Christians can certainly write about what we do know.

If God is glorified by excellent art, and if we are commanded to give our attention to things that are true, lovely, pure, and praiseworthy, then what are we supposed to do when the culture around us produces things that are ugly, sloppy, sinful, or full of lies? Does merely complaining about it help? Certainly not. Neither does producing art that speaks truth but is of poor quality. No, Christians must produce God-honoring art that is excellent, lovely, pure, and true.

How are we to do this? First, we must start with studying God's Word. Next, we must also study excellent and beautiful art, wherever we find it. Preaching is good for Sunday, but with art, *showing* is usually better than *telling*. We must present stories that demonstrate the truth. And we must not shy away from difficult subjects but address them from God's perspective, as the Bible does. We must learn from all good art and produce works that glorify our heavenly Father, through our Lord Jesus, by the power of the Holy Spirit.

★ ★ ★ A Prayer for America ★ ★ ★

Heavenly Father, Your Word tells us that every good and perfect gift is from above, coming down from You. Help me to find the good, the true, and the beautiful wherever it is. Help me to shun mediocrity, impurity, and falsehood and to strive for excellence in everything. I know that art done with skill brings glory to You. Wherever Your Spirit breathes, there life, truth, and beauty burst forth. Fill me with the Holy Spirit to create or to appreciate works of art that glorify You. In Your name I pray, Lord Jesus. Amen.

★　★　★

He has filled them with skill to perform every work of
an engraver and of a designer and of an embroiderer,
in blue and in purple and in scarlet material,
and in fine linen, and of a weaver, as performers
of every work and makers of designs.

—Exodus 35:35

27

For Gratitude

In October 1863, there seemed little to thank God for. The United States had been torn in two in a bloody civil war since February 1861, and over three hundred thousand Americans had already died in the fighting, with another million injured. Although the North had superior numbers and resources, many of their generals were incompetent. Victory seemed nowhere in sight, even after two and a half years of carnage. The very existence of the Republic stood in question.[1]

In the shadow of all this bloodshed and anxiety, what did President Abraham Lincoln do? He called for a day of thanksgiving! In Lincoln's Thanksgiving Proclamation, he said to a weary and divided nation:

The year that is drawing toward its close has been filled with the blessings of fruitful fields and healthful skies. To these bounties, which are so constantly enjoyed that we are prone to forget the source from which they come, others have been added, which are of so extraordinary a nature that they cannot fail to penetrate and soften even the heart

which is habitually insensible to the ever watchful providence of almighty God.[2]

Was Lincoln delusional? Was he insensitive to the massive loss
of life? Was he burying his head in the sand?

No, Lincoln knew full well the human cost of the war. He
understood the challenges that faced the fragile republic. But he
also understood an important principle for happiness, godliness,
and success: We always have something to give thanks for—usually
much more than we think.

In the midst of the storm, Lincoln saw the silver lining. He
realized that things could have been much worse. And he thanked
God for His hand of providence, restraining evil, providing for their
needs, and protecting them. He continued, "No human counsel
hath devised, nor hath any mortal hand worked out these great
things. They are the gracious gifts of the most high God, who while
dealing with us in anger for our sins, hath nevertheless remembered
mercy."[3]

What amazing words of gratitude! Lincoln recognized the consequences for sin but also God's amazing grace shown to them.
This allowed Lincoln to take his eyes off of himself and to focus on
others.

President Lincoln closed his 1863 Thanksgiving Proclamation
with these words:

I recommend to them [American citizens] that, while offer-
ing up the ascriptions justly due to him for such singu-
lar deliverances and blessings, they do also, with humble
penitence for our national perverseness and disobedience,
commend to his tender care all those who have become
widows, orphans, mourners, or sufferers in the lamentable

civil strife in which we are unavoidably engaged, and fervently implore the interposition of the almighty hand to heal the wounds of the nation, and to restore it, as soon as may be consistent with the Divine purposes, to the full enjoyment of peace, harmony, tranquility, and union.[4]

What about today? Are we Americans so self-absorbed that we forget to give thanks to God or to help those less fortunate? Our nation is divided on many issues, but we face no open violence. Our creature comforts and security have increased dramatically since the 1860s. Smallpox and polio have been defeated in America. Life expectancy has gone up. Child mortality has gone down. Slavery and Jim Crow laws have been eradicated, and communication has become immediate.

But what do you and I so often do? We focus on ourselves. We complain when someone cuts us off in traffic instead of rejoicing that we own a car. We grow impatient at slow internet service instead of marveling at the miracle of smartphones. And we pout when God doesn't give us everything we want instead of falling on our knees and thanking Him for meeting our needs—especially our need for grace and mercy.

If our nation is going to stand firm in our faith and be a beacon of hope to the world, then we must demonstrate lives that are overflowing with gratitude. We must focus not on our visible circumstances but on the invisible God who is in control of those circumstances. As Paul said in 2 Corinthians 4:18, "Look not at the things which are seen, but at the things which are not seen; for the things which are seen are temporal, but the things which are not seen are eternal."

When we regularly express gratitude to God for what He has done, when we continually take inventory of all the good things

God has done for us, then we will be less likely to wander away from God. After all, why would we want to leave the One who is the source of all the blessings in our lives? Instead of looking around at what other people have and coveting those things, thank God for what He has given you.[5] Trust in His unique plan for your life and focus on what God values most. The truth is, God owes you and me nothing except eternal condemnation for our sins. But thanks be to God that He does not give us what we deserve!

Ingratitude and envy are tearing our nation apart. We cannot constantly demand that the government give us the property of those who own more than we do. Instead, we must develop an attitude of thankfulness.

Make a list of things to be grateful for. Whenever you are tempted to complain, look at your list, and thank God for an item on that list. Keep updating the list. And try to find someone less fortunate whom you can bless this week. Believe me, developing these godly habits will increase your joy and contentment. And if enough Americans make these habits part of their daily lives, we would have much less civil strife and much more unity.

✶ ✶ ✶ A Prayer for America ✶ ✶ ✶

Heavenly Father, thank You for the many blessings You have poured out on me and our nation. We do not deserve them. Help Americans all across this great land—including me—to choose to be thankful, rather than ungrateful, demanding, or entitled. Thank You for food and shelter. Teach me to be content with that. Everything else is a bonus. Lord, You do not owe us anything except punishment for our sins. But Your Word says You richly give us all things to enjoy, including forgiveness for our sins through Your Son, Jesus Christ, who died on the cross in our place to give us eternal life with You. What greater gift could there possibly be? You are so good to us, heavenly Father. Help us to love others as you have loved us. In Jesus' name I pray. Amen.

* * *

Rejoice always; pray without ceasing;
in everything give thanks; for this
is God's will for you in Christ Jesus.

—1 Thessalonians 5:16–18

28

For Forgiving Others

Frederick Douglass came into this world sometime in February 1818. Slaves were forbidden from keeping records, so Douglass never knew the exact date of his birth. Given the name Frederick Bailey, he was born on the eastern shore of Maryland, on one of the twenty-five plantations owned by Colonel Edward Lloyd.[1]

Frederick's mother was a slave named Harriet Bailey. His father was a white man, most likely the master who managed the one thousand slaves on Lloyd's estates. White slave masters often raped their female slaves, populating Southern plantations with mixed-race children like Frederick.

Frederick was ripped from his mother's arms when he was just an infant and sent to Holmes Hill Farm, miles away, where his maternal grandmother, Betty Bailey, raised him. After a backbreaking day of work, Harriet would sometimes walk to Frederick's cabin and sing him to sleep.

"Good night, my little Valentine," she would whisper in his ear as she tucked him into bed. Because of his mother's goodnight blessings, Frederick adopted February 14 as his birthday. Harriet would then walk the miles back to her plantation to sleep for a few hours before going back into the fields. Years later, Frederick recalled that he never saw his mother in daylight.

At seven or eight, Frederick was taken away from his grandmother and sent to work at another plantation and then for Lloyd's extended family in Baltimore. While in the city, his masters as well as others taught Frederick to read, even though it was against the law. Soon, Frederick found speeches about the natural rights of man described in the Constitution. The more Frederick read, the more he loved the Constitution and the more he came to realize how much he had been wronged by slavery.

About this same time, a Methodist preacher led Frederick to Christ, and another man mentored him in the Lord. But in 1833, Frederick was taken back to the plantation. Frederick was fifteen, and he now belonged to Lloyd's son-in-law, Captain Thomas Auld. Auld was cruel and stingy, beating and starving slaves who did not please him. Frederick began fighting back, so Auld sent the "troublesome" Frederick to a local farmer for "retraining." This farmer was merciless and extremely cruel. But one day, Frederick fought back against him as well, and the tyrant never bothered him again.

Later, Frederick conspired to escape North, but his plan was discovered. He could have been sold downriver, but God was with him, and he was instead sent back to Baltimore. There, he met Anna Murray, a free black woman. They fell in love, escaped to the North, and married. To prevent being kidnapped and stolen back South, Frederick changed his last name to Douglass. He and Anna eventually had five children together.

Frederick loved his country, and he used his considerable writing and speaking skills to proclaim the biblical dignity of every human, which was outlined in the Constitution. After the Civil War, the Thirteenth, Fourteenth, and Fifteenth Amendments to the Constitution were ratified. Much work remained to be done, but black people had finally won their rights.

In the meantime, Frederick had gained honor and prestige for his work, including being named the grand marshal of Washington, DC. At that time, he received an invitation to visit his old master Thomas Auld. Auld was in his eighties, frail and near death. Painful memories flooded Frederick's mind. Yet Frederick knew that Jesus Christ had forgiven him of all his sins, and he had to do likewise.

So Frederick agreed and traveled to the old plantation full of ghosts from the past. He was soon escorted to see Thomas.

"Captain Auld," he greeted his former master.

"Marshal Douglass," the old man rasped.

Frederick was stunned. *My old master is addressing me with my title of respect.*

"Not Marshal, but Frederick to you as formerly," he said as he walked over to the side of the bed and took up Auld's trembling hand. Frederick had already forgiven Auld. He now had compassion for him.

Auld died shortly after Frederick Douglass's visit. Frederick could have let past wrongs make him bitter, but he sought for reconciliation whenever possible.

Each of us has been wronged in many ways—some of us more than others. In fact, some have had to endure unspeakable injustice. But the truth is, even the worst things that another person can do to us are small compared to how we have sinned against God. In Matthew 18:24–28, Jesus compared the sin debt we owe to God as hundreds of thousands of times worse than the sin debt that others owe us! And if we have trusted in Jesus' death and resurrection, then God has forgiven us of all of it. In fact, God is constantly forgiving us. We must do the same for others.

You may think it's impossible to forgive that person who has wronged you. Let me offer some clarity to help ease your mind. Forgiving someone is not excusing their sin or letting them hurt you again. And forgiveness is not excepting them from legal consequences. Bringing a criminal to justice may be the best thing for them and for society. Instead, forgiveness is taking your hands off their throat and trusting their fate to God. However, if you refuse to forgive someone, that shows that you have not yet accepted God's forgiveness for you. You cannot give what you have not received. Each of us must forgive one another from the heart. When we forgive, we release a prisoner, and we find that the prisoner was us.

Right now in America, many people sit in the self-made prison of unforgiveness. Much of the vitriol we see on the news or read about online comes from people who have not forgiven others. Many vent their hatred against those they feel have wronged them, not seeing their own flaws or need for forgiveness from God. Unforgiveness makes our nation nastier, less safe, and more divided. Only by forgiving others can we reconcile many of our differences. Pray that Americans see their sins against God and accept His forgiveness in Jesus Christ. And pray that we then forgive one another, for our own sins against God are far worse than what others have done to us. But when we place our faith in Jesus Christ, God promises to forgive us completely.

✶ ✶ ✶ A Prayer for America ✶ ✶ ✶

Heavenly Father, many of us have endured terrible wrongs at the hands of others. But Your Word tells us that even the greatest sin anyone can commit against a fellow human is small compared to the way we have wronged You. Yet You freely give us forgiveness, Lord Jesus. What amazing grace! Help me to fully grasp Your pardon and to extend that same forgiveness to others. I know that forgiveness is not excusing people's sins, bailing them out of consequences, or allowing them to keep hurting me. But forgiveness is taking my hands off of their necks, leaving justice to You. Thank You, Lord Jesus, for paying for all my sins on the cross. In Your name I pray. Amen.

* * *

If you forgive others for their transgressions,
your heavenly Father will also forgive you.
But if you do not forgive others, then your Father
will not forgive your transgressions.

—MATTHEW 6:14–15

For Wisdom

The name's Lafayette. James Lafayette. America's first double agent. And a slave.

James was born as property to William Armistead in Virginia, sometime in the mid-1700s. The exact year of his birth is not known, since slaves were not allowed to keep records.

Under British colonial law, James had only forced servitude and degradation to look forward to for the rest of his life. But stirrings of freedom were blowing. Pamphlets from the Puritan pastor John Wise proclaiming the God-given dignity of every human being according to God's Word were being spread throughout the thirteen colonies. In 1776, the Continental Congress used language from his pamphlet to write the Declaration of Independence, making the dangerous decision to separate from England. It was either do or die for these patriots.

James believed in the biblical ideals of freedom, justice, and equality. While many slaves were escaping to join the British, in 1781, James volunteered to join the US Army. He had been faithful, even under unjust circumstances, so his master granted him permission to join the army with the last name of Armistead. The Continental Army stationed James to serve the French general, the

Marquis de Lafayette, whose forces were assisting the Americans in Virginia.

Lafayette quickly recognized that James had a special advantage: He was a black slave who could also read and write (many British assumed that all slaves in North America were illiterate). James had also proven himself to be very cunning and wise. Because of this, Lafayette made the risky decision to ask James to spy for them. James agreed.

Shortly thereafter, James "wandered" into the British camp, claiming to be a runaway slave, and offered to serve their cause. The British suspected nothing and assigned James to help their general, Charles Cornwallis. Since he knew the Virginia landscape, James offered to help the general as a spy. Cornwallis agreed. In this way, James was able to move freely between the American and British camps. He would give the British flawed data but provide the Americans with detailed intelligence. He was America's first double agent, and he was good. The British never suspected a thing.

Soon, James was assigned to help none other than the turncoat Benedict Arnold. Arnold had been a skilled colonial soldier, but he felt that he had been disrespected by the Continental Congress. After being placed in command at West Point, Arnold decided to betray his countrymen for promises of wealth and prestige from the British. He planned to sell the fort of West Point to them and help assassinate George Washington. But through a miraculous string of circumstances, Arnold's treachery was discovered, and he fled. The British then made Arnold a general and placed him in command of British troops and German mercenaries who were fighting against the Americans in Virginia. Arnold openly spoke of his battle plans in front of James and foolishly left important maps and documents uncovered in his presence. James took notes and relayed the valuable British battle plans back to the Americans and French.

Using the details of James's reports, Generals Lafayette and

Washington were able to blockade and surround the British at Yorktown, Virginia. This timely action caught the British off guard. After three weeks of constant bombardment, the British officially surrendered on October 19, 1781. The war was effectively over. James's fearless espionage saved countless American lives and helped win American independence.

Despite his heroic and priceless contribution, James was forced to return to slavery after the war. In a 1783 law for slave-soldiers, the Virginia General Assembly had stated that every slave who fought for the cause of American independence was entitled to their own freedom. But that same assembly claimed that James was not eligible because technically he was not a slave-soldier but a slave-spy.

James refused to give up, and he petitioned the Virginia legislature. His old friend the Marquis de Lafayette heard of his struggle and wrote a letter recommending freedom for the loyal soldier. The request was finally granted in 1787. In gratitude, James adopted "Lafayette" as his new last name. He went on to buy forty acres, began farming, got married, and raised a large family. In 1818, the Virginia legislature awarded James Armistead Lafayette a yearly pension of $40 (around $809 in today's money) for the rest of his life for his service.

In 1824, the Marquis de Lafayette returned to America to visit the nation he helped liberate. He was welcomed as a hero by thousands in all twenty-four states at the time. While passing through a town in Virginia, he spotted James in the crowd. The nobleman jumped from his carriage, pushed through the throng, and embraced his friend.

James Armistead Lafayette died on August 9, 1830, a wealthy and respected man.[1] Benedict Arnold, in contrast, fled to England but never received the wealth and position he was offered. His name has forever become synonymous with *traitor*.

We all need wisdom in our lives. We all face pressures and

injustices that could make us or break us. Pray for wisdom, not only for yourself but also for your fellow Americans. Since we live in a democratic republic, the wiser our fellow voters are, the stronger our nation will be. From big decisions to small, we must all learn to respond to the pressures of life with God's perspective. If we do so, we can rise from even terrible circumstances to accomplish God's glorious mission for us, a mission that will echo into eternity. If we do not, then we can fall even from a position of privilege to become a byword for all time: "The memory of the righteous is blessed, but the name of the wicked will rot. The wise of heart will receive commands, but a babbling fool will be ruined" (Prov. 10:7–8). Be a James Lafayette, not a Benedict Arnold.

⋆ ⋆ ⋆ A Prayer for America ⋆ ⋆ ⋆

Heavenly Father, our nation needs wisdom today. Give America's leaders wisdom as they make decisions, and grant wisdom to our citizens as we seek to honor You in our daily lives. Whenever we face injustice or difficulties, help us to respond with Your perspective. I realize that the potential for greatness, and for great evil, lies within every person, including me. Show me the right path, and give me the courage to take it. Thank You, Father, that in Christ Jesus—the embodiment of wisdom—You have given every Christian the Holy Spirit, which is the Spirit of wisdom. For You promise that if we ask You in faith, You will gladly give us wisdom. In Jesus' name I pray. Amen.

⋆ ⋆ ⋆

If any of you lacks wisdom, let him ask of God,
who gives to all generously and without reproach,
and it will be given to him.

—JAMES 1:5

For Discernment

In the 1730s and 1740s, God spread the fire of revival across the thirteen colonies in America. This revival came to be known as the Great Awakening. Most preachers at the time were scholarly and stoic. They were not given to outbursts of emotion. However, during the Great Awakening, many people in the pews would weep or wail from conviction of sin and fear of hell. After a sermon, some would sing or dance to celebrate that they had been saved by Jesus. A few would even make animal noises! Revivalist Jonathan Edwards had great discernment. He wrote that some of these displays of emotion were genuinely of the Spirit, while others—such as barking like a dog—were distractions from Satan. However, he noted that the overall results of the revival were salvation for thousands and renewed interest in the Bible.[1]

After America won its independence from Britain, a new generation longed for—and prayed for—a revival like they had heard about from their grandparents. It came in the 1790s and lasted for forty years. From New England to the Western frontier, thousands of people repented of their sins and came to Christ. Just like the first Great Awakening, this Second Great Awakening was accompanied by wailing and singing. However, fainting, crying out, and making animal noises became much more common. And unlike the first Great Awakening, many preachers this time were less scholarly but more animated and confrontational in their preaching—perhaps none more so than Charles Grandison Finney.

Finney was born in 1792 in Connecticut but moved with his family to upstate New York when he was two.[2] As a young man, he apprenticed to become a lawyer and earned his law license. In 1821, however, he had a dramatic experience in the woods and dedicated his life to evangelism.

Two years later, Finney began preaching. Finney revolutionized revival services. He pioneered the altar call (or the "anxious seat," as he called it), where people would come down front during a service to indicate that they had made a commitment to God. Finney would also publicly rebuke people by name in his sermons and prayers.[3] His preaching became famous, and he eventually taught beyond upstate New York in large cities both in America and in Britain.

Finney was also active on social issues. He supported the Underground Railroad. In 1835, he became a professor at Oberlin College in Ohio, and from 1851 to 1866, he served as its president. Oberlin was the first college in America to accept women and black students along with white men.

Finney has been regarded as a hero by many evangelicals, including Dwight L. Moody, Billy Graham, and Greg Laurie. There's just one problem.

Charles Finney was a heretic.

That term is not too strong. For instance, Finney taught that Jesus died on the cross not to pay for our sins but to show how seriously God took sin so that we would live moral lives. Finney also denied that Christ's righteousness is imputed to any who trust in Him. Finney denied original sin and taught that people are capable of living perfectly. In fact, Finney said that we must become perfect in this life if we hope to get into heaven.

Finney cloaked his heresies in Christian terms.[4] To him, being "born again" meant to follow Christ's example of obedience. In other words, you—not the Holy Spirit—must regenerate yourself. "Salvation" was not a miracle, he said, but was simply applying the right circumstances to an individual to get the right results.[5] If you sinned again after "salvation," then you were lost again until you repented and began living righteously again.[6]

These heresies are a far cry from what the Bible actually teaches. And they are dangerous for a person's eternal soul. For instance, according to Romans 5:12, we have all inherited a sin nature because of Adam's sin in the garden of Eden: "Through one man sin entered into the world, and death through sin, and so death spread to all men, because all sinned." We are all born with the sin virus. Because of this, we all sin and continue to accumulate a sin debt with God. And since God is holy, He must punish that sin.

But as 1 John 2:2 says, "He Himself [Jesus] is the propitiation for our sins." That word *propitiation* means appeasement or satisfaction. In other words, Jesus appeased the justified wrath that God felt for our many sins, by taking our sins upon Himself and paying for them on the cross with His own death. As Paul said in 2 Corinthians 5:21, "He [God the Father] made Him [Jesus] who knew no sin to be sin on our behalf, so that we might become the righteousness of God in Him."

So, how do we "become the righteousness of God in Him"? By faith: "For by grace you have been saved through faith; and that not of yourselves, it is the gift of God; not as a result of works, so that no one may boast" (Eph. 2:8–9). When we place our faith in Jesus for our salvation, He not only takes our sin on Himself, but He also gives us His righteousness. He then makes us born again by the Holy Spirit of God: "He saved us, not on the basis of deeds which we have done in righteousness, but according to His mercy, by the washing of regeneration [being born again] and renewing by the Holy Spirit" (Titus 3:5).

Being born again is a miracle from God that gives us new desires to do righteous deeds, which results in us doing good works: "For we are His workmanship, created in Christ Jesus for good works, which God prepared beforehand so that we would walk in them" (Eph. 2:10). These good works are the result of our being born again, not the cause of them.

However, although we gain new desires, we still retain many of our old desires. This new born-again nature struggles with our old sin nature for the rest of our lives. A mature Christian is not sinless, but he or she will sin less and less over time. And although we will struggle with the sin nature until the day we die, God assures us that a Christian can never lose his salvation: "For those whom He foreknew, He also predestined to become conformed to the image of His Son, so that He would be the firstborn among many brethren; and these whom He predestined, He also called; and these whom He called, He also justified; and these whom He justified, He also glorified" (Rom. 8:29–30).

As you can see, Charles Finney was desperately wrong on all these vital doctrines. And these issues are not secondary. They are critical for a person's eternal destiny.

"But Finney produced good fruit," you may protest. It's true; he did promote some good causes. But wherever Finney preached, people soon became so disillusioned with his sanctified self-help—masquerading as the gospel—that they grew immune to Christianity. Indeed, the area where Finney preached the majority of his messages in New York is called the "burned-over district," because false teaching like his made it fireproof to real revival. One contemporary of Finney's said, "During ten years, hundreds, and perhaps thousands, were annually reported to be converted on all hands;

but now it is admitted, that real converts are comparatively few. It is declared, even by [Finney] himself, that 'the great body of them are a disgrace to religion.'"[7]

This "burned-over district" became fertile soil for deception. Almost every major cult in America sprung from this region during Finney's preaching, or shortly thereafter. These groups use deceptively Christian terms but deviate from Christ's gospel.[8]

Today, we face the same situation. False teachers who promise to "name it and claim it" disguise their errors in positive slogans or Christian-sounding terms. We must be discerning so that we can tell true movements of the Spirit from false ones. Pray for discernment, and become firmly rooted in God's Word.

★ ★ ★ A Prayer for America ★ ★ ★

Heavenly Father, give us discernment as a nation. As Jesus said in John 7:24, may we not judge by surface appearances, but help us to make right judgments. Many false teachers have gone out, both being deceived and deceiving others. Help me to know the true gospel and to be grounded in Your Word, so I can share it with others and not be fooled myself. In Jesus' name I pray. Amen.

★ ★ ★

Examine everything carefully;
hold fast to that which is good.

—1 THESSALONIANS 5:21

For Personal Repentance

Growing up in Boston during the Great Depression, Chuck Colson met many destitute people. Even during his youth, he was driven to make the world a better place for them. During World War II, young Colson raised enough money in his middle school to buy a Jeep for the US Army. He was the first person in his family to go to college, and he did so on an academic scholarship, graduating in 1952 with honors from Brown. He served as a US Marine officer in 1953 in the Korean War, achieving the rank of captain in just two years. He worked for the assistant secretary of the US Navy and then went to law school at night while serving as the youngest administrative assistant to a US senator. He graduated law school with honors and founded a highly successful law firm. But he left that lucrative career in 1969 to become special counsel for the Nixon administration to make a greater impact.

Colson was driven and brilliant, and he believed his actions were improving the world. His office was directly next to the president's in the White House. Colson was so tough that he was known as Nixon's "hatchet man." He advised the president every day, and in 1972, he helped Nixon win reelection by the largest margin in American history. At age forty-one, Colson had achieved the pinnacle of his career. However, he felt sad and empty. He left the administration in 1973 to go back to private practice.

Soon after, he ran into a former client and friend whom he hadn't seen in years. This man had recently become a Christian at a Billy Graham crusade. Chuck noticed a difference in his life, and so they met again. This time his friend read a chapter to Colson from C. S. Lewis's *Mere Christianity*. It was the chapter on pride. As his friend read, Chuck realized that while many of his actions were done to help others, he also had an inflated view of himself. He had fooled himself into thinking that everything he had done was for his country. But now he realized that much of it had been for his own advancement and ego. After his friend finished reading, he led Chuck in a prayer to trust in Jesus as his Savior. For the first time in his life, Chuck was convinced that there was a God who cared about him.

And he lived happily ever after, right? Not yet! In March 1974, Chuck was indicted and called to testify before Congress for his part in the Watergate scandal. He realized that he was innocent of the specific crime presented against him but was guilty of a different crime. For the first time in his career, he didn't try to make excuses for it. He confessed his sins to God and accepted Christ's forgiveness. But there was still something he needed to do.

Against his lawyers' advice, Colson walked into the prosecutor's office and pled guilty to the crime he wasn't even charged with but of which he was guilty. He knew that he had to come clean and let go of his old life. So, in July 1974, at the age of forty-three, Chuck Colson went from an office in the White House to a prison cell.

His sentence was short: seven months. But the experience changed him. His fellow inmates—murderers, thieves, drug dealers—men he formerly would have looked down on, became his brothers. "I'm no better than they are," he realized.[1] He grew to love them and held a regular Bible study with them. He also noticed injustices in the criminal justice system. He believed God wanted him to do something for prisoners and their families once he got out. So he resolved to help however he could.

Chuck received many good job offers upon release in 1975. But he turned them down. He had just written the book *Born Again,* and he used the royalties from it to begin Prison Fellowship in 1976. Little did he know that his life was just beginning.

Prison Fellowship has since become the nation's largest outreach to convicts, ex-convicts, and their families. It has fifty thousand volunteers in America and is now present in 120 other countries. Colson also began other ministries, such as BreakPoint, Angel Tree, and Justice Fellowship. Each Christmas, Angel Tree delivers gifts to five hundred thousand children whose parents are incarcerated.

Colson accomplished much prison reform but also cultural and academic reform. In 1994, he helped orchestrate the *Evangelicals and Catholics Together* ecumenical document, and in 2009 he signed the Manhattan Declaration, calling on Christians not to comply with laws that violate God's principles. During his lifetime, Colson wrote more than a dozen books and received numerous awards and honorary degrees. He worked until he went home to be with the Lord on April 21, 2012.

Although he achieved incredible accomplishments by worldly standards in the first half of his life, Chuck Colson really achieved significance once he gave his life to Jesus and repented of his sins. If he had taken his lawyers' advice, doing what some involved in the Watergate scandal did—not admitting their guilt or accepting responsibility—then he never would have gone to prison, found forgiveness, or found his life purpose.[2]

Many Americans today do exactly that. They make all sorts of excuses to explain away their sin: "It's my parents' fault." "Everyone back then was doing it." "The system is biased against me." Others try to justify their actions by saying that the ends justify the means.

Still others have gotten away with their sins for so long, they have deadened their consciences and don't even bother making excuses.

The truth is, many external factors hurt us and tempt us to sin. But at some point, each of us has to take responsibility for our own part in sin. And then we must accept the good news of God's forgiveness in Christ Jesus. This is the only way forward. And it is the only way to national revival. Pray that millions of Americans do this exact thing.

Some of you reading right now have a sin in your life that you need to repent of. Some of you need to seek the forgiveness of someone else also, besides that of God. It's a painful action to take but a necessary one. You may experience temporal consequences, but you can leave the results with God. If you have trusted in Jesus for the forgiveness of your sins, then God will use even your mess-ups and your screw-ups for good. But delaying repentance will only make things worse. Proverbs 28:13 says, "He who conceals his transgressions will not prosper, but he who confesses and forsakes them will find compassion."

God is full of mercy and compassion. He is ready and waiting to forgive you of all of your sins right now. And He is ready to give you a new start.

★ ★ ★ A Prayer for America ★ ★ ★

Heavenly Father, I know that I am a sinner who deserves Your righteous wrath. But because of Your amazing love and grace shown to me in Jesus Christ, I can have my sins forgiven and paid for on the cross. What's more, You can redeem every pain and mistake from my past. But I must admit my sin to You and accept responsibility for it. Help me repent quickly when I sin. And help us as a nation to repent of our sins and turn to You. You say that if we hold on to our lives, we will lose them. But if we lose our lives for Your sake, Lord Jesus, then we will find true life. Forgive us, cleanse us, and use us for Your glory to bless others and to experience fullness of life. In Jesus' name I pray. Amen.

★ ★ ★

If we confess our sins, He is faithful
and righteous to forgive us our sins
and to cleanse us from all unrighteousness.

—1 JOHN 1:9

For Those Deceived
by False Religions

A man once claimed to receive special revelation from an angel of God in a cave. This angel told the man that Christians and Jews had gotten their message wrong and had corrupted the Scriptures. This angel now delivered God's "correct revelation," which supposedly superseded prior revelations. Thus, this man became God's "prophet" of the true religion of Abraham.

This prophet eventually wrote his message in a holy book and began preaching it. He received converts but also resistance. The man traveled around with his followers, sometimes being persecuted and sometimes persecuting others. They attempted to take over the politics and economy of every area they spread to. Sometimes open violence broke out.

This prophet claimed God said it was good to have multiple wives, and he even married a child bride—something many of his followers still practice today. This prophet also taught that people must work for heaven and that eternal sex with many women is a reward in heaven. He forbade alcohol and taught that Jesus is not eternal God but was created just like every other man. He taught that Jesus lived an exceptionally holy life and thus earned heaven, and we can as well.

Eventually, the followers of this new prophet moved into a desert location, where they set up their religion around a central building. They established a strict theocracy and even murdered a peaceful caravan passing through, except for a few young children. Eventually, this group grew into the millions, due in large part to polygamy and high birth rates. Also, this man was light-skinned, and he associated black Africans with the work of the devil.

Who am I talking about? If you said Muhammad, you would be right![1] But if you said Joseph Smith, you would also be right! The parallels between these two false prophets are staggering, even though they contradict each other in the specifics of their so-called revelations from God.

Satan has no new tricks up his sleeves. His deceptions vary in detail, but over the millennia, he has used the same basic set of lies to try to keep people from God. As the apostle John said, "Beloved, do not believe every spirit, but test the spirits to see whether they are from God, because many false prophets have gone out into the world" (1 John 4:1).

Those who are deceived by false religions are headed for an eternity of punishment, separated from God, unless they trust Jesus for forgiveness. Today, the claim that there is only one way to God draws abuse from many in America. "How arrogant! How hateful!" they say. But these same critics ignore the fact that many of the world's religions claim that they are the only way. They can't all be right.

Jesus said, "Enter through the narrow gate; for the gate is wide and the way is broad that leads to destruction, and there are many who enter through it. For the gate is small and the way is narrow that leads to life, and there are few who find it" (Matt. 7:13–14). Jesus also said, "I am the way, and the truth, and the life; no one comes to the Father but through Me" (John 14:6). Many modern leftists would decry Jesus as a bigot if they met Him on the street today. But God is under no obligation to provide many ways to heaven. He has graciously provided one way to be saved from sin. God loves us so much that He sent His Son, who became flesh, died on a cross, and paid our sin debt. He then rose victoriously from the dead on the third day (1 Cor. 15:1–4).

Every false religion gets this wrong:

1. Every false religion claims that you must work for your salvation ("Do!"). Christianity teaches that Jesus has already earned our salvation completely for us ("Done!").

2. Many false religions distort the goodness of God. They either claim that God is capricious (like in Islam) or that He does not care about sin (like many liberal "Christians").

3. Many false religions deny the truth about the afterlife. They either deny the bodily resurrection (materialists), or they deny that we live only once and then face judgment (such as Hindus, Buddhists, and Scientologists).

4. Finally, every false religion distorts the person and/or work of Jesus Christ. Christianity teaches that Jesus is the eternal Son of God, the Second Person of the Trinity (the other members of the Trinity are God the Father and God the Spirit). Jesus has always existed and has always been God (John 1:1–4). Jesus became fully man and was born of the Virgin Mary, while still remaining God (John 1:14; Luke 2). That is how He is able to pay for all of our sins by dying on the cross and then rising physically from the grave: He is the God-Man. Many false religions give lip service to Jesus (such as

Mormonism, Islam, and Jehovah's Witnesses), but they deny who He really is.

Right before Jesus was taken up to heaven, He said, "All authority has been given to Me in heaven and on earth. Go therefore and make disciples of all the nations, baptizing them in the name of the Father and the Son and the Holy Spirit, teaching them to observe all that I commanded you; and lo, I am with you always, even to the end of the age" (Matt. 28:18–20). In America, we are blessed to have pretty much all nations and faiths brought to us. We have neighbors from all over the world and from every religion imaginable. And they may be great people by worldly standards. But if they have not placed their trust in Jesus as revealed in the Bible for the forgiveness of their sins, then they are headed to an eternity separated from God. God may have placed them near you for a reason. Ask God to remove the veil from their eyes. And ask God to help you share the gospel with them, gently correcting any misconceptions they may have about Jesus. And remember, Jesus is "with you always, even to the end of the age."

★ ★ ★ A Prayer for America ★ ★ ★

Heavenly Father, Your Word says that Satan comes to steal, kill, and destroy. He has blinded the eyes of unbelievers. Father, please remove the veil from their eyes to see the glory in Christ Jesus, Your only begotten Son. Bring them to spiritual life to see the truth of Your Word by the Holy Spirit. Prick their conscience over sin and their need for a Savior. May they see Your love shining in me, and may I be ready to share the reason for my hope with gentleness and respect. Thank You for saving me, and through Your Holy Spirit, save those around me. In Your name I pray, Lord Jesus. Amen.

★ ★ ★

He who believes in Him [Jesus] is not judged;
he who does not believe has been judged already,
because he has not believed in the name
of the only begotten Son of God.

—JOHN 3:18

For Bible Literacy

O ur forefathers came to this country from diverse religious backgrounds. Some, we are often told, were Christians, and others were deists (believing that God made this universe and then left it alone), but most were secularists who believed that religion was fine as long as it was confined to the church and home. Supposedly our nation's founders were determined to build an unscalable wall of separation that would keep any religious influence from seeping into public life.

Yet that version of American history belongs in the same category as George Washington and the cherry tree: It is pure myth. Most of our nation's founders were deeply influenced by biblical thought, and many were devout Christians. Far from embracing deism, the vast majority believed in a God who regularly intervened in human affairs. And they *all* wanted Christian principles of morality taught and promoted in the public square.[1]

Why? Because they knew that the foundation of our nation's laws must be the eternal principles found in the Bible. They designed America's brilliant system of government not on Enlightenment ideas but mainly on precepts gleaned from the Bible.[2]

An examination of two of our nation's supposedly deist founders will illustrate this. When the Continental Congress debated what America's new motto and seal should be, both Thomas Jefferson and Benjamin Franklin suggested an image of Moses leading the Israelites out of Egypt, with God's glory shining out of the pillar of cloud and the Red Sea swallowing up the Egyptian army. Around the seal, both Jefferson and Franklin wanted the words "Rebellion to tyrants is obedience to God." The Bible clearly impacted their political theory.

The Bible also affected their policy. When Jefferson was governor of Virginia, he called for a day of Thanksgiving to "Almighty God,"[3] and Franklin believed the Continental Congress should begin their session seeking the favor of God. In Philadelphia on June 28, 1787, Franklin said,

> I have lived, sir, a long time and the longer I live, the more convincing proofs I see of this truth—that God governs in the affairs of men. And if a sparrow cannot fall to the ground without his notice, is it probable that an empire can rise without his aid? We have been assured, sir, in the sacred writings that "except the Lord build they labor in vain that build it." I firmly believe this; and I also believe that without his concurring aid we shall succeed in this political building no better than the Builders of Babel: We shall be divided by our little partial local interests; our projects will be confounded, and we ourselves shall become a reproach and a bye word down to future age.[4]

In this short speech, Franklin alluded to at least five separate Bible passages. Franklin knew his Christian Bible well.[5] He also flatly denied a key tenet of deism by stating that "God governs in the affairs of men," and they must seek His aid if they hoped to succeed in forming a workable nation. Franklin's idea of God is much more in line with what the Bible teaches than with the deistic god of Enlightenment thought.

Clearly, knowledge of the Bible greatly influenced these two brilliant men. The eternal truths found in God's Word will help establish a just society, but that is only its secondary purpose. God gave us the Bible primarily to know of His perfect will, to find salvation in Jesus, and to grow in the grace and knowledge of our Lord Jesus Christ. Society is changed when enough people in that society have become transformed by the power of the Holy Spirit through faith in Jesus Christ.

Two more American Founding Fathers illustrate this point: Elias Boudinot and John Jay. Elias Boudinot was a delegate from New Jersey to the Continental Congress and served as its president from 1782 to 1783. He was later appointed by George Washington to be the first director of America's national mint, which he ran from 1795 to 1805. John Jay was a delegate from New York and also served as president of the Continental Congress from 1778 to 1779. John Jay was also the key negotiator for the Treaty of Paris, which ended the Revolutionary War, was the first chief justice of the Supreme Court, and was our first ambassador to Spain.

These are just some of the many accomplishments of these esteemed men. But perhaps nothing these patriots accomplished had a more lasting effect than their founding and presiding over the American Bible Society in 1816. In their words, they wanted to "distribute the Bible, 'without note or comment,' to as many people as possible," because "the message of the Bible could transform lives and set the nation on a proper moral course."[6] And they lived out God's Word in their own lives. Both men were faithful in their families and churches, and both men tirelessly worked to end slavery in their states. John Jay concluded, "No human society has ever been able to maintain both order and freedom, both cohesiveness and liberty apart from the moral precepts of the Christian Religion. Should our Republic ever forget this fundamental precept of governance, we will then, be surely doomed."[7]

Today, sadly, we seem to have forgotten our biblical roots. Bible literacy is at an all-time low. Fewer than half of all adults can name all four Gospels. Sixty percent of Americans can't name five of the Ten Commandments, and only 43 percent can name the first five books of the Bible.[8] The situation is not much better with Christians. Less than half of those who regularly attend church read the Bible more than once a week, and almost one in five say they never read it. This biblical ignorance leads to dangerous heresy: 59 percent of evangelical Christians believe the Holy Spirit is not a personal Being but a force, like in *Star Wars!*[9]

No wonder our nation is so godless. We have become unmoored from our biblical foundation. Certainly, some churches bear the blame. Sanctified psychology preached from the pulpit cannot substitute for solid Bible teaching. But the primary responsibility of educating children about the Bible falls on parents. As Albert Mohler, president of Southern Baptist Theological Seminary, says, "Parents are to be the first and most important educators of their own children, diligently teaching them the Word of God…God assigned parents this nonnegotiable responsibility, and children must see their Christian parents as teachers and fellow students of God's Word."[10]

If you are a parent, be sure to instruct your children in the Bible and to encourage Bible memorization. Many wonderful children's Bibles exist to help you in this most important task. If your own parents did not teach you about Scripture, don't fret. It's never too late. Make it a personal practice to get into the Bible and memorize Scripture for yourself every day. You don't have to read much, maybe even just a few verses at a time. Think about those verses, and ask your heavenly Father to help you put into practice what He is teaching you. Maybe even follow a daily Bible reading plan. And if you don't understand what a specific verse is saying, find a good Bible teacher to help explain it to you.

Finally, pray that God renews our national interest in His Word. If enough people would take in God's Word like their daily meals and try to live by it, then our nation would be transformed in unbelievable ways.

★ ★ ★ A Prayer for America ★ ★ ★

Heavenly Father, You have given us the priceless gift of Your Word, the Bible. Help me to cherish this love letter from You and view it as my daily bread. Use the words of Scripture, Holy Spirit, to transform me into the image of Jesus Christ. Increase Bible literacy in my life, in my home, in other homes across the nation, in churches, and in our civilization as a whole. In Your name we pray, Lord Jesus. Amen.

★ ★ ★

Let the word of Christ richly dwell within you,
with all wisdom teaching and admonishing
one another with psalms and hymns and
spiritual songs, singing with thankfulness
in your hearts to God.

—COLOSSIANS 3:16

For Courageous Pastors

What makes America great? Is it our military strength? It is our prosperity? Is it our freedom?

Even in the early 1800s, people wanted to know. So, in 1831, the French government sent sociologist Alexis de Tocqueville to study America.[1] He spent nine months traveling the United States, observing our prisons, churches, politics, industry, art, and economy. When he returned to France, Tocqueville wrote his observations in a massive tome titled *Democracy in America*. It took him eight years to write, and it was released in two volumes. It has since become a classic.

Tocqueville recognized that the earliest Puritan pastors established the bedrock idea of social equality: Everyone is royalty. He also noted how later American clergy built on this idea and taught that the Christian faith leads to liberty. This concept was foreign in Europe. But in America—by contrast—during the Revolutionary era, it was the clergy who most advocated for independence from Britain. Influenced by the recent revival known as the Great Awakening, these pastors did not shy away from applying God's Word to current events. Their bold, biblical teaching fueled the fire of freedom. Except for the Anglican churches (which were funded by Britain), the vast majority of pastors in America preached against British rule without representation and for independence.[2]

And Britain took notice. In 1776, Ambrose Serle, the secretary to British general William Howe in New York, wrote that the American Revolution was ultimately a religious war.[3] King George III, loyalists in America, and the English aristocracy all referred to the war as a "Presbyterian Rebellion."[4] Although the title of "Presbyterian" was a bit oversimplified, it did reveal that Christian pastors played a large part in America's struggle.

And many of those pastors paid a high price for their support of the revolution, losing their property or even their lives. Speaking truth always carries a price. But the eternal rewards far outweigh it. As the apostle Paul said in 2 Corinthians 4:17, "For momentary, light affliction is producing for us an eternal weight of glory far beyond all comparison."

These pastors gave the colonists the courage to govern themselves. Later, many of these same pastors fought against slavery. Boldly preaching God's Word gave America its strength. Tocqueville noted this in his lengthy book. But, coming from France, he also noted—from experience—what would happen if pastors ever stopped preaching biblical truth:

> When the religion of a people is destroyed, doubt gets hold of the higher powers of the intellect and half paralyzes all the others. Every man accustoms himself to having only confused and changing notions on the subjects most interesting to his fellow creatures and himself. His opinions are ill-defended and easily abandoned; and, in despair of ever solving by himself the hard problems respecting the destiny of man, he ignobly submits to think no more about them.
>
> Such a condition cannot but enervate the soul, relax the springs of the will, and prepare a people for servitude.

Not only does it happen in such a case that they allow their freedom to be taken from them; they frequently surrender it themselves.[5]

In other words, if we abandon God's Word, we fall into bondage. The apostle Paul wrote in Galatians 5:1, "It was for freedom that Christ set us free; therefore keep standing firm and do not be subject again to a yoke of slavery." This principle applies to every sphere of life.

Pastors today are facing immense pressure to water down the biblical message. "Keep quiet on social and political issues," they hear. "Your job is only to preach the gospel!" But pastors who separate the Bible from real life are not being faithful to preach the "whole purpose of God" (Acts 20:27). Such abandonment will ultimately undercut the power of the gospel message.

On the other hand, if pastors do speak out on politics or culture, groups like the American Civil Liberties Union (ACLU) or Americans United for the Separation of Church and State will try to intimidate them and their churches from attempting to influence legislation and elections. During my thirty-five years of ministry, I have taken well-publicized stands against homosexuality, abortion, and discrimination against Christians. I have been threatened with physical violence and with the loss of our church's tax-exempt status by the ACLU and other like-minded groups.[6] But let me tell you a little secret: No church has ever lost its tax-exempt status for speaking on politics. And even if it did, that would be no reason for the church to cower and keep silent. Jesus has called us to be salt and light in the world.

Do you want to make America great? Do you want to remain free? Then pray for pastors to boldly preach God's Word. Ask God to give them discernment and courage to apply the Bible to every area of life. Encourage them to promote godliness and to oppose evil. Ask God to protect them from every one of Satan's schemes and temptations. And for yourself, find a Bible-believing church, and listen to your pastor. Follow him as he follows Christ. Live out what he teaches you from the Word. For "Righteousness exalts a nation, but sin is a disgrace to any people" (Prov. 14:34). This is the Bible's prescription for making any nation great.

Finally, pastors, be brave. Speak winsomely, boldly, and in love. Your flock needs you. And when the Chief Shepherd returns, He will reward you.

★ ★ ★ A Prayer for America ★ ★ ★

Heavenly Father, motivate pastors in America to boldly preach the truth in love. Give them courage. Give them wisdom and skill to rightly divide Your Word. May Christians across our nation support godly pastors and not make their jobs any harder than necessary. And may we apply their biblical teaching to every area of our lives—including my own. In Your name I pray, Lord Jesus. Amen.

★ ★ ★

I solemnly charge you in the presence of God
and of Christ Jesus, who is to judge the living
and the dead, and by His appearing and
His kingdom: preach the word; be ready in season
and out of season; reprove, rebuke, exhort,
with great patience and instruction.

—2 TIMOTHY 4:1–2

For Churches

In May 1942, the Axis Powers (Germany, Italy, and Japan) controlled most of Europe, North Africa, the Pacific, and East Asia. Their united evil seemed unstoppable. Europe was deemed "Fortress Europe" by military experts, and Japan had not lost a single battle up to that point.

But then the tide of World War II began to shift. On June 6, 1942, the United States won the Battle of Midway. Japan never won a battle after that. On September 8, 1943, Italy surrendered to the Allies, and on June 6, 1944, Fortress Europe was breached. More than 150,000 American, British, and other Allied troops sailed one hundred miles across the rough English Channel to invade Nazi-occupied France. These brave men—of whom the average age was twenty-one—manned over six thousand ships. This invasion, dubbed Operation Overlord, was the largest amphibious attack in history.

On the morning of D-Day—as June 6 came to be called—President Franklin D. Roosevelt went on radio to address the nation. He described what was happening to his fellow Americans and led them in prayer:

Almighty God: Our sons, pride of our nation, this day, have set upon a mighty endeavor, a struggle to preserve our Republic, our religion and our civilization and to set free a suffering humanity. Lead them straight and true; give strength to their arms, stoutness to their hearts, steadfastness in their faith.

They will need Thy blessings. Their road will be long and hard. For the enemy is strong. He may hurl back our forces. Success may not come with rushing speed, but we shall return again and again; and we know that by Thy grace, and by the righteousness of our cause, our sons will triumph.

And God heard their prayer. By the end of August, northern France was liberated. By the following spring, the Third Reich had fallen, and on September 2, 1945, Japan surrendered.[1]

Sometimes it feels as if the forces of evil in our world are unstoppable. But that is an illusion. God has already written the last chapter, and He has created a spiritual army to combat evil until He returns. We may not always see it, but Christ's kingdom is advancing all the time, soul by soul. And one day, Jesus Christ will return with His heavenly invading force and will destroy the powers of wickedness: "The armies which are in heaven, clothed in fine linen, white and clean, were following Him on white horses. From His mouth comes a sharp sword, so that with it He may strike down the nations, and He will rule them with a rod of iron; and He treads the wine press of the fierce wrath of God, the Almighty" (Rev. 19:14–15). This mighty spiritual army—this unstoppable invading force—is called the church.

So, what are the characteristics of a healthy church? This is important to know if we are to be effective. First, a healthy church follows the right directives. God left us with our marching orders until He returns: the Bible. Make sure you are a part of a church that believes in, teaches, and tries to obey the Bible as God's inspired, infallible, authoritative Word. We all fall short, but a healthy church lovingly tries to put God's Word into action.

Second, find a church that shows genuine love and grace. Many churches have correct doctrine but do not show compassion to outsiders or even to insiders. They have become legalistic and have forgotten that they themselves are sinners who have been saved by God's grace. A church like this has left its first love: "I know your deeds and your toil and perseverance, and that you cannot tolerate evil men, and you put to the test those who call themselves apostles, and they are not, and you found them to be false…But I have this against you, that you have left your first love" (Rev. 2:2, 4).

Third, a healthy church seeks to save the lost. Many in this world live as enemies of God, and they will face His righteous wrath unless they turn to Jesus before He returns: "Go therefore and make disciples of all the nations, baptizing them in the name of the Father and the Son and the Holy Spirit, teaching them to observe all that I commanded you; and lo, I am with you always, even to the end of the age" (Matt. 28:19–20).

Fourth, find a church that engages in heartfelt worship of God the Father, Son, and Holy Spirit. Love for the Savior should permeate every aspect of our lives. Don't get caught up on specific worship styles, but instead look to see if the words are based in Scripture and come from hearts of gratitude: "Let the word of Christ richly dwell within you, with all wisdom teaching and admonishing one another with psalms and hymns and spiritual songs, singing with thankfulness in your hearts to God" (Col. 3:16).

Fifth, look for a church that deals biblically with sin and conflict. The church is made up of imperfect people, so problems will arise. Additionally, a wolf in sheep's clothing will occasionally slip in among the flock, and the pastors will have to protect the other sheep. These are unpopular tasks, but they are necessary for the health of Christ's body: "Brethren, even if anyone is caught in any trespass, you who are spiritual, restore such a one in a spirit of gentleness; each one looking to yourself, so that you too will not be tempted" (Gal. 6:1).

Finally, do not look for a perfect church. No such organization exists. The church is made up of sinners who have been convicted of their sins, rescued, born again, and are in the process of being renewed. For such people God enlists into His army. And we all serve faithfully, side by side, as we together wait for our Commander and King, Jesus Christ, to return and to establish His perfect kingdom on earth.

The church is an outpost of heaven, which has established a beachhead here on earth. And we Christians are called to be active in this "household of God, which is the church of the living God, the pillar and support of the truth" (1 Tim. 3:15). The stronger and healthier our churches are, the stronger and healthier our nation will be. America has been blessed by Bible-believing churches since her inception. This has made her great. And if we want our nation to be strong, then we need to pray for—and be a part of—Christ's body on earth, that unstoppable force: the church.

★ ★ ★ A Prayer for America ★ ★ ★

Heavenly Father, You have enlisted me into the kingdom and army of Your Son, my Lord and Savior, Jesus Christ. Thank You, Lord Jesus, that while I was Your enemy, fighting against You, You died for me. You have made me a part of Your heavenly army—the church. And You have called the church to wage spiritual warfare against spiritual enemies. Help us to be an outpost of heaven, here on earth. As the church, we wait for and long for Your glorious return when You will vanquish evil and usher in perfect righteousness. Come quickly, Lord Jesus. In Your name I pray. Amen.

★ ★ ★

He is clothed with a robe dipped in blood,
and His name is called The Word of God.
And the armies which are in heaven,
clothed in fine linen, white and clean,
were following Him on white horses.

—REVELATION 19:13–14

36

For Victory in
Spiritual Warfare

In the spring of 2003, American troops stormed through Iraq to depose that nation's brutal dictator, Saddam Hussein.[1] They met with stunning success. All along the way, however, Hussein's minister of information, Muhammad Saeed al-Sahhaf, kept broadcasting to the Iraqi people that their military was decimating American forces. Even when US troops marched through the center of the capital, Baghdad Bob—as al-Sahhaf came to be known—declared, "There is no presence of American columns in the city of Baghdad at all."[2]

Satan is similar to Baghdad Bob. Even though Jesus defeated Satan at the cross and his ultimate demise is fast approaching, the devil still tries to blind unbelievers in America and throughout the world to the reality of Christ's advancing kingdom. He even tries to deceive Christians—who are more than conquerors in Christ Jesus—into leading defeated lives. Satan wants to destroy America and to destroy you personally.

To accomplish his goals, Satan has personalized a blueprint for each person's destruction. Although everyone is different, Satan usually includes three strategies to bring you down.

First, Satan tries to discourage you from worshipping God. All of heaven praises the Lord and watches to see if you will do the same. Supremely prideful, the devil wants to convince humans to stop worshipping the Lord. One way he attempts this is through trials and discouragement. Satan tries to use financial pressure, family conflicts, health issues, or even the death of a loved one to turn you away from God.

Second, Satan tries to distract you from serving God. He wants to create as much distance as possible between you and your Creator. In twenty-first-century America, we have more opportunities for diversion than at any other time in history. Most of these diversions are not sinful in and of themselves, but we cannot let temporary concerns choke out our passion for God. In the parable of the soils, Jesus compares distracted people to thorny soil (Luke 8:14). Jesus lists three types of spiritual weeds that can strangle out our desire for God:

1. *Worries.* Satan often plants fears in our minds to scare us from following God in faith. We must realize that most of the things we worry about never happen. They are based on lies, placed there by Satan, whom Jesus described as "a liar and the father of lies" (John 8:44).

2. *Riches.* Those of us who live in the United States are some of the wealthiest people on earth.[3] Now, there is nothing wrong with riches. But we must watch out that the pursuit and maintenance of wealth does not make us unfruitful in God's service. Jesus said, "You cannot serve God and wealth" (Matt. 6:24). Riches are a distraction not only to those who have an abundance of financial

resources but also to those who have a lack. Most people are worried that they have too little money, fearing they won't have enough to meet their future needs. They think if they had just a little more, then they would be happy. But Jesus said, "Your heavenly Father knows that you need all these things. But seek first His kingdom and His righteousness, and all these things will be added to you" (Matt. 6:32–33).

3. *Pleasures of this life.* Jesus does not condemn enjoyment. In fact, pleasure—kept in balance—can draw us closer to God if we thank Him for it. As Paul wrote in 1 Timothy 4:4, "Everything created by God is good, and nothing is to be rejected if it is received with gratitude." The devil, however, tries to lure us into becoming preoccupied with pleasure. He will either try to get us to abstain from pleasure or to worship pleasure; either extreme plays into our enemy's plan.

Third, Satan tries to deceive you into directly disobeying God. In James 1:14–15, we see Satan's temptation equation:

Corrupt Desires + Right Bait + Wrong Choice = Sin

We all have normal, God-given desires, such as the desire for recognition, intimacy, sex, power, and possessions. There is nothing wrong with wanting any of these. The problem comes when we try to satisfy our natural desires in our own way—as Adam and Eve did—rather than trusting God's way. Ever since the first couple's fall in the garden, the inclination toward sin has become part of us. And Satan plays on our corrupt desires.

Next, Satan uses the right bait. We do not all crave the same forbidden fruit at the same time or to the same extent. Like any good fisherman, Satan observes us, chooses the best lure, and dangles it before us at the best time. He usually chooses moments when we have experienced great success, when we are tired, when we are alone, or when we are waiting on God. Jesus experienced all these conditions when Satan tempted Him in the wilderness, as recorded in Matthew 3:16–4:11. Jesus had recently experienced a great spiritual triumph at His baptism, He was exhausted from forty days of fasting, He had been isolated for forty days, and He was waiting on God to give Him the go-ahead to begin His ministry—a ministry that would end with His death on the cross. It was at this time that Satan tempted Jesus. But Jesus resisted and won with the Word of God.

Finally, sin happens when we choose to take Satan's bait. Choice is the factor over which we have the most control. Our corrupt desires do not force us to sin. Neither do Satan's lures. We cannot completely control either of those, but we can control our responses.

Satan cannot snatch God's children out of His hand. But he will try to discourage you from worshipping, from serving, and from obeying God. However, if you are in Christ, God has given you the power to resist temptation. The Bible says that the same power that raised Jesus from the grave is now at work in your life, giving you the ability to say no to temptation and to "walk in newness of life" (Rom. 6:4).

So, how do you as an individual, and we as a nation, walk in this newness of life? First, pray that God makes you aware of how Satan is trying to tempt you personally. You must know your enemy's schemes if you are to fight him. Second, as Paul said in Ephesians 6:10–18, use the armor of God to combat the devil, praying "at all times in the Spirit." Third, pray for your fellow Christians who are experiencing the same attacks. As believers, we all have spiritual targets painted on our backs. Finally, pray that God opens the eyes of all Americans to see their need for a Savior and to realize the spiritual battle they are in.

If enough Americans will follow these steps, then Satan's attacks on them individually, as well as on our entire nation, will have about as much effect as Baghdad Bob shouting into a broken TV camera.

★ ★ ★ A Prayer for America ★ ★ ★

Heavenly Father, though I may not always realize it, I am always in a war with the devil, the enemy of my soul. He works through deceived people as well as my own corrupt desires to bring me down and to oppose Your perfect purposes. Thank You, Father, that no one can snatch me out of Your hands if I have trusted in Jesus for salvation. But Satan seeks to steal my joy, kill my witness, and destroy some of my eternal rewards. Help me—as well as other Christians throughout our nation—to resist the devil through prayer, Scripture memorization, obedience, and Christian fellowship. In Jesus' name I pray. Amen.

★ ★ ★

Our struggle is not against flesh and blood,
but against the rulers, against the powers,
against the world forces of this darkness,
against the spiritual forces of wickedness
in the heavenly places.
—EPHESIANS 6:12

37

For Steadfastness in Persecution

In 2012, two men walked into the Masterpiece Cakeshop in Lakewood, Colorado, and asked the owner, Jack Phillips, to design a cake for their wedding. Jack is a Christian who chooses not to make custom cakes for Halloween, divorce celebrations, bachelor parties, or other events or messages that he feels conflict with his love of Jesus. So, Jack politely declined and suggested they buy one of his premade cakes or visit one of the many other bakeries in the area that would service their needs. Instead, the couple sued Jack. Not only that, but the State of Colorado also sued Jack. They slandered him with all sorts of terrible labels, as did much of the media.[1]

After six long years, Jack's case wound up in the Supreme Court. In a seven-to-two decision, the Court ruled in his favor. But the very next day, a person called Jack's bakery to demand a cake celebrating a sex-reassignment surgery. Jack refused that as well, and he was again sued by his state. This time, Jack countersued, and finally, in 2019, the State of Colorado dropped their suit against him. A few months later, Jack was sued again by the same person!

Persecution from the LGBTQ+ community and from the State of Colorado has cost Jack hundreds of thousands of dollars in legal fees, thousands of hours away from his business, and much anxiety over the possibility of losing his passion and profession.

While Jack was defending his faith in the US court system, his fellow Christians across the world at Zion Church in Sri Lanka were experiencing a different kind of persecution. On April 21, 2019—Easter morning—Sunday school teachers led their class of around thirty children in a lesson on Christ's resurrection. They asked these children if they would be willing to die for Jesus. All the kids said yes. Moments later, seven Muslim suicide bombers blew themselves up—one at Zion Church and six at two other Christian churches and three hotels in the area. These jihadis killed over three hundred people that day—mostly Christians, including twelve of those children—and wounded another five hundred people.[2]

Persecution comes in many forms and levels of intensity. It can range from slander and harassment to torture and murder. But it is all suffering for the sake of Christ. And Jesus told us this would happen. He said in John 15:18, "If the world hates you, you know that it has hated Me before it hated you." He continued in verse 20, "Remember the word that I said to you, 'A slave is not greater than his master.' If they persecuted Me, they will also persecute you."

Ever since Stephen was martyred for Christ in Jerusalem, as recorded in Acts 7:54–8:3, Christians have been persecuted wherever the gospel has spread. In fact, the gospel has sometimes spread because of persecution. As the Christian leader Tertullian wrote in the second century, "The blood of martyrs is the seed of the church."[3]

Indeed, this persecution and spread of the church continues today. At this very moment Christians around the globe are enduring severe persecution. Every month, an average of 345 Christians are murdered for their faith, 105 churches and Christian buildings are burned or attacked, and 219 Christians are arrested, detained without trial, and/or sentenced and imprisoned for Christ.[4] Faced with such devastating statistics, we might be tempted to think that Satan is winning! But in Matthew 16:18, Jesus promised, "I will build My church; and the gates of Hades will not overpower it."

Here in America, you and I may never be killed or imprisoned for our faith—or we might. We will certainly be slandered as "hateful" or "intolerant" if we obey Christ. We may even be sued, harassed, or fined. As our culture increasingly loosens its ties to our nation's Christian heritage, we should expect growing hostility toward those who attempt to stem the tide of evil sweeping our land by "holding fast the word of life" (Phil. 2:16).[5]

Persecution is painful, but it is a sign that we are living out our faith in this world. As the apostle Paul said in 2 Timothy 3:12, "All who desire to live godly in Christ Jesus will be persecuted." And persecution earns for us a blessing if we endure through the trial. James 1:12 says, "Blessed is a man who perseveres under trial; for once he has been approved, he will receive the crown of life which the Lord has promised to those who love Him."

We overcome persecution not only by relying on the power of God but also by praying for our persecutors, for we were once God's enemies as well. Jesus put it this way in Matthew 5:44–45: "Love your enemies and pray for those who persecute you, so that you may be sons of your Father who is in heaven."

Christ is our ultimate example of one who was slandered, tortured, and killed for righteousness, but He loved His enemies until the end.

Maybe someone has lied about you or called you nasty names for standing up for righteousness or for God's Word. Maybe a friend or loved one refuses to speak to you or excludes you for your faith. Or maybe others have done worse. Or maybe you have never really endured any persecution for Christ. Regardless, the Bible says that all Christians will endure some level of persecution for following Him. And right now, millions of our brothers and sisters in Christ are experiencing intense persecution for following Jesus. Pray for their safety, encouragement, and endurance. Pray that their persecutors repent and trust in Jesus, before it is too late for them. Consider supporting groups that aid the persecuted church, like Voice of the Martyrs or Open Doors USA. If you yourself have been persecuted for Christ's sake, rejoice that God has found you worthy to suffer for Jesus! Forgive your persecutors, and ask God to forgive them and bring them to repentance and salvation. And remain in a body of believers through a local church. We are meant to go through the trials of this life together.

⋆ ⋆ ⋆ A Prayer for America ⋆ ⋆ ⋆

Heavenly Father, all over the world, my brothers and sisters in Christ face persecution, torture, and even death for the sake of Your Son, Jesus Christ. Grant justice for the persecutors and healing for the persecuted. I trust that what others mean for evil, You will use for good. Father, empower all Your people—including me—to love our enemies, to do good to those who hate us, and to pray for those who mistreat us. Provide for the needs of Your people all over the world. May their persecutors repent before Your wrath comes upon them. Thank You for the religious liberty we enjoy here in America. May I and my fellow citizens use our freedom to love You and love others well. And may we continue to love well even if we are also called on to suffer. Unite us as one body as we weep with our brothers and sisters who are suffering—sharing in the fellowship of Your suffering and looking forward to sharing in the power of Your resurrection. In Jesus' name I pray. Amen.[6]

* * *

Blessed are you when people insult you and
persecute you, and falsely say all kinds of evil
against you because of Me. Rejoice and be glad,
for your reward in heaven is great;
for in the same way they persecuted
the prophets who were before you.

—MATTHEW 5:11–12

Against Spiritual Blindness

On March 24, 1820, Frances Jane Crosby was born in Brewster, New York. She was a beautiful, healthy baby. But when she was six weeks old, she caught a cold, as babies often do, and her eyes became inflamed. A quack convinced her parents that he was a doctor and blinded her by applying the wrong treatment to her eyes. A few months later, Frances's father died, and her mother was forced to work as a maid. Thankfully, Frances's Christian grandmother helped raise little Fanny, as Frances came to be known.

Fanny's grandmother instilled in her a love of Scripture, a love of poetry, and a heart of gratitude to Jesus. Fanny herself displayed an amazing recollection, memorizing five chapters of the Bible every week! She also showed a superb talent for poetry. At age eight, she wrote her first poem:

Oh, what a happy soul I am,
although I cannot see!
I am resolved that in this world
Contented I will be.

How many blessings I enjoy
That other people don't,
To weep and sigh because I'm blind
I cannot, and I won't!

Shortly before her fifteenth birthday, Fanny was sent to the newly formed New York Institute for the Blind. One of her teachers thought that writing poetry was a waste of time and that it dishonored God. Thankfully, a visiting scholar met Crosby and told her instructors, "Here is a poetess. Give her every possible encouragement. Read the best books to her and teach her the finest that is in poetry. You will hear from this young lady someday."[1]

His words proved prophetic. By age twenty-three, Fanny was reading her poems to Congress, writing verses for dignitaries, and hobnobbing with US presidents.

When Crosby was thirty-eight, she married the brilliant organist Alexander van Alstyne, who was also blind. He wrote music to accompany many of her poems. Fanny learned to play the harp, piano, guitar, as well as other musical instruments. Soon, famous musicians began seeking Fanny's collaboration, including William Howard Doane. Doane was a brilliant inventor, philanthropist, and accomplished composer. He stopped by Fanny's home unannounced one day with a tune he had recently written. He was supposed to perform a new song at a Sunday school convention in another town. However, the train for that town was departing in thirty-five minutes, and he could think of no words! Fanny agreed to help, and Doane quickly sat down at the piano and played the tune.

"Your music says, 'Safe in the Arms of Jesus,'" Fanny blurted out, and she scribbled down a hymn. "Read it on the train and hurry. You don't want to be late!" she said as she pushed him out the door.[2] The hymn has since become one of her most beloved.

In addition to her teaching job and philanthropy work, Fanny was under contract to submit three hymns a week to her publisher, but she often wrote six or seven a day. She could write incredibly complex songs and compose music with a more classical structure if she wanted to. In fact, she wrote at least five cantatas, including *The Flower Queen*, America's first secular cantata. But Fanny preferred to write simple verses that could be used for evangelism. The great gospel preacher D. L. Moody used her songs in his crusades. Fanny died on February 12, 1915, at the ripe old age of ninety-four.

During her incredibly productive life, Fanny Crosby wrote and published four books of poetry, two autobiographies, at least five cantatas, several eulogies for dignitaries, and many speeches, both for herself and for others. She did all this in addition to her teaching career and charity work. But none of this compares to her hymns.

Crosby ended up writing and publishing between eight thousand and ten thousand hymns—in addition to numerous secular songs. This makes Fanny Crosby the most prolific songwriter ever—not in American history, not in the history of the English language, but in the history of earth! No one else comes even close. She wrote so many hymns that she used around two hundred pseudonyms so that her name would not dominate church hymnals. (She wrote under so many pen names that we are not sure exactly how many hymns are really hers. But most believe it is near nine thousand.) Over one hundred million copies of her songs have been printed.

Fanny is best remembered today for her hymns. Among her creations are such beloved classics as "Blessed Assurance," "Saved by Grace," "To God Be the Glory," "Pass Me Not, O Gentle Savior," "Safe in the Arms of Jesus," and "All the Way My Savior Leads Me." Although she was blind, Fanny Crosby could see spiritual realities that most sighted people could not.[3]

Today, we see the opposite. You can state seemingly obvious truths like "men are not women," "killing babies for convenience is murder," and "Jesus Christ is the only way to be saved," and many will flatly deny it. They may even label you as "hateful," a "racist," or a "Nazi."

The Bible calls this condition spiritual blindness. Like a malicious quack, the god of this world—Satan—has blinded many people to the truth: "And even if our gospel is veiled, it is veiled to those who are perishing, in whose case the god of this world has blinded the minds of the unbelieving so that they might not see the light of the gospel of the glory of Christ, who is the image of God" (2 Cor. 4:3–4).

The devil has whispered in the ears of the lost things that appeal to their own prejudices and sin nature, and they latch on to it. We are all susceptible to this condition. Only by the grace of the Holy Spirit can spiritual blindness be truly cured: "For God, who said, 'Light shall shine out of darkness,' is the One who has shone in our hearts to give the Light of the knowledge of the glory of God in the face of Christ" (2 Cor. 4:6).

Pray that God opens the eyes of those who are spiritually blind. Pray that they see their own need for a Savior, God's love for them, and God's provision in Jesus Christ. And pray that they place their faith in Christ alone for eternal life. The future success of our nation depends on our spiritual sight—on Americans placing their faith in Jesus. And once our short lives on this planet are over, our eternal destiny depends on it. For one day, our amazing nation will end. But God's perfect kingdom will last forever.

Perfect submission, all is at rest,
I in my Savior am happy and blest;
Watching and waiting, looking above,
Filled with His goodness, lost in His love.
—Fanny Crosby, "Blessed Assurance"

★ ★ ★ **A Prayer for America** ★ ★ ★

Heavenly Father, You sent Jesus into the world to open the eyes of the blind and to save the lost. Lord, I know that the physical blindness You healed on earth points to the much deeper spiritual blindness we are all born with. Unless You healed me, I would not have seen the glory of God in Your loving face either, Lord Jesus. Thank You for opening my eyes so that I could see the truth and be saved. Lord Jesus, give spiritual sight to the millions of people in America who are spiritually blind and don't even know it. In Your name I pray, Lord Jesus. Amen.

★ ★ ★

The Spirit of the Lord is upon Me,
Because He anointed Me to preach
the gospel to the poor.
He has sent Me to proclaim release
to the captives,
And recovery of sight to the blind,
To set free those who are oppressed,
To proclaim the favorable year of the Lord.

—LUKE 4:18–19

For Revival

Spiritual revival comes from the preaching of superstar evangelists, right? When we consider the great national revivals throughout America's history, we usually think of famous evangelists such as Jonathan Edwards, D. L. Moody, and Billy Graham. Many Christians today are looking for another charismatic orator to bring godliness and spiritual renewal to our nation.

But does revival come only from preachers? Let's consider the answer to that question using a story from America's past.

In 1857, the North Dutch Church in New York City had been slowly losing members. To reverse this trend, the church hired forty-nine-year-old clothing merchant Jeremiah Lanphier to evangelize local businesses. Lanphier faithfully executed his duties, but the church saw no improvement.

At this time, America was prosperous, but religious life had declined. Preachers such as William Miller had declared that the world was going to end in the 1840s. When that did not happen, many became disillusioned with Christianity and turned to alcohol or financial speculation. A quiet desperation dogged those who hustled about, looking for riches and pleasure.

Noticing this angst, Lanphier prayed, "Lord, what would You have me to do?" He believed that God responded, "I want others to enjoy an active prayer life."

So Lanphier opened a meeting hall on Fulton Street for one hour a week. He hoped businesspeople would gather and pray during their lunch hour. He set the first meeting for September 23, 1857, and distributed flyers all over Manhattan.

However, at the first meeting, only six men showed up. *What a lackluster response*, Lanphier thought. Then Christ's words from Matthew 18:20 came to mind: "Where two or three have gathered together in My name, I am there in their midst."

Lanphier didn't complain or quit, but he thanked God for the response. He then led the half dozen men in prayer. The following week, twenty men showed up; the week after that, forty.

God heard their prayers, but not in the way they expected. On October 14, the stock market crashed. Banks in New York closed— and stayed closed for two months. The men at the meeting begged to meet more often, and Lanphier booked the hall for seven days a week. Soon, three thousand people a day flocked to the prayer meetings! More prayer meetings popped up all over Manhattan. Within six months, more than ten thousand businessmen in New York City were gathering every day for prayer.

In February 1858, the *New York Herald* gave extensive coverage to the movement. Not to be outdone, the competing *New York Tribune* devoted an entire issue in April 1858 to the revival. This, along with the newly invented telegraph, spread the revival out west. In Chicago, two thousand people met every day in the Metropolitan Theatre to pray, and the same number met every day in downtown Cleveland. In St. Louis, churches were filled with prayers daily for months on end, and in Louisville, Kentucky, several thousand met daily for prayer. In some cities, tents were set up to accommodate the numbers, and the newly formed Young Men's Christian Association (YMCA) held prayer meetings in their locations.

Throughout 1858, pastors all over America were baptizing twenty thousand new believers every week. By 1859, the revival had spread to Canada, Great Britain, and beyond.

This movement was led by laypeople, not church leaders or orators. It became known as the Businessmen's Revival. In America alone, an estimated one million people were added to church membership, and as many as one million more church members became saved. One out of every twelve lost Americans turned to Jesus! All of this happened because an ordinary businessman prayed faithfully, and God heard his prayers.[1]

The same is true today. We do not need to wait for God to bring around the next Billy Graham. We need to start with ourselves. Revival begins when we follow several steps. First, trust the work of Jesus on the cross for your own forgiveness and salvation, if you have not already done so. Second, repent of any known sins in your life. Third, dwell on God's Word—the Bible—every day. Next, become connected to a local body of believers—the church. Fourth, in response to what the Spirit is telling you in His Word and through biblical preaching, daily connect to Him in prayer. Pray about everything. When we pray in accordance with God's will, He promises to give us what we ask for (1 John 5:14–15). And we know that God's will is to see the lost saved. Finally, look for ways to minister to those around you. If you follow these steps, I promise you that God will use you. And who knows, He might even use you to bring about His next great revival.

⋆ ⋆ ⋆ A Prayer for America ⋆ ⋆ ⋆

Heavenly Father, our nation needs You now as much as ever. Please bring revival to America. Give people throughout our nation a hunger for holiness and for Your Word. Thank You for calling me, and every Christian, to be salt and light in this world. Forgive me of my sin and apathy, and help me to walk according to Your Spirit. Thank You for Your amazing grace and forgiveness. May I never take it for granted. To You be all the glory. In Jesus' name I pray. Amen.

⋆ ⋆ ⋆

Thus says the high and exalted One
Who lives forever, whose name is Holy,
"I dwell on a high and holy place,
And also with the contrite and lowly of spirit
In order to revive the spirit of the lowly
And to revive the heart of the contrite."

—Isaiah 57:15

For Evangelism

Right now, in America, we have more opportunities for ministry and evangelism than at any other point in human history. Advances such as the internet, airline travel, and disposable income enable us to share God's Word as never before.

God often uses moments of great opportunity to spread the gospel. Jesus Christ came at the perfect time for the rapid growth of the church. The Romans had established peace throughout their empire, they had built roads for quicker travel, and most of the empire understood the common language of Greek. As the apostle Paul—the greatest evangelist in history—said, Christ came in "the fullness of time" (Gal. 4:4).

We see God's hand creating other moments of great potential in history that Christians seized upon. The Byzantine Empire fell in 1453, which caused many Eastern scholars to flee to Western Europe. They brought with them thousands of Greek biblical texts, which led Protestant reformers like Martin Luther, Ulrich Zwingli, and John Calvin to look at the original biblical texts. During this time, Johannes Gutenberg invented the printing press in Germany. This allowed Martin Luther, in the 1500s, to spread gospel ideas rapidly and made it easier for Bibles to be printed in a person's native language. In fact, the first major book that Gutenberg printed on his press was the Gutenberg Bible.

The Reformation ideas of salvation by grace alone, through faith alone, in Christ alone, as revealed in Scripture alone, to the glory of God alone then spread to Great Britain, where they took hold. Britain then spread the gospel throughout their empire. This process continued in Britain's greatest colony: America. After the original thirteen colonies broke off from England and became the United States of America, we began expanding the reach of the gospel even more. Three Americans invented the single-circuit telegraph in the 1830s. In 1844, they sent their first message: "What hath God wrought!" (Num. 23:23 KJV).

The telegraph soon spread across America and then the world. The telegraph was critical in expanding the Businessmen's Revival across America, Canada, and Britain in 1857–58.

In 1903, American brothers Orville and Wilbur Wright completed the first successful manned flight. Christians quickly took advantage of the new technology of air travel and sent missionaries, Bibles, and gospel resources across the globe.

On Christmas Eve, 1906, the first ever audible radio broadcast was given from Brant Rock, Massachusetts. In part, it consisted of the Christmas carol "O Holy Night," as well as the proclamation of Christ's arrival: "Fear not: for, behold, I bring you good tidings of great joy, which shall be to all people. For unto you is born this day in the city of David a Saviour, which is Christ the Lord" (Luke 2:10–11 KJV).

The first sermon was broadcast over radio from Wichita, Kansas, in May 1920, six months before the first commercial radio station opened its doors. I am proud to share that my church—First Baptist Church of Dallas, Texas—was a pioneer in radio evangelism. In 1921, we began broadcasting then pastor George Truett's sermons, all the way until his death in 1944. Pastor W. A. Criswell then took over and, in 1951, became one of the first pastors to broadcast his sermons using the brand-new American-invented technology of television.

All these advancements came together with First Dallas's most famous church member, Billy Graham. In 1948, Billy Graham led his first crusade in Los Angeles. It was going poorly until media mogul William Randolph Hearst sent a two-word telegram to all his newspapers: "Puff Graham." The next day, Billy Graham was on the front page of every one of Hearst's papers. Other papers, magazines, and radio stations soon followed suit, and the rest is history. Through the advancements of air travel, Billy Graham went on to speak before over 215 million people in 185 countries and territories—more than anyone else in history. And those were just his live appearances. Add in radio, TV, and cinema, and during his lifetime, Billy Graham shared the good news of salvation in Jesus Christ to well over a billion people.

And the God-given opportunities for spreading the gospel continue. In the 1960s, the US Department of Defense developed ARPANET, which would eventually lead to the internet we have today. Now, almost anyone in the world can access almost any information instantaneously.

Still, the Great Commission is not complete. There are still people on this planet who have not yet heard the gospel. But we are getting close. And with the peace, prosperity, technology, and mobility that many people around the world enjoy today, we Christians could reach all nations on earth within our generation. But we have no idea how long God will allow this window to remain open.

God never intended for the ministry of evangelism to be confined to paid professionals. Instead, He wants every Christian to be in the game. Why? The majority of non-Christians will never come through the doors of a church to hear about the saving power of Jesus Christ. That is why the primary strategy of the early church for spreading the gospel of Jesus Christ was not "come and hear" but "go and tell." If we are serious about appearing as lights in the world, then every Christian must be both willing and able to take the message of Christ from the church into our neighborhoods, schools, places of work, and relationships.

As Christians, we are to use every opportunity that God gives us to pierce the darkness of our culture with the light of His Word. And all believers across America are called to be faithful, wherever God has placed us, to use the time, talent, and treasure that God has given us to make disciples of all nations.[1]

Ask God to give you opportunities to share the gospel with lost people around you. Ask your heavenly Father to give you the right words to say, and then trust Him with the results. And pray that God would open even more doors across our nation, so Christians can continue to share the good news of salvation in Jesus Christ.

★ ★ ★ A Prayer for America ★ ★ ★

Heavenly Father, like the believers who came before us, help Christians across America to fulfill the Great Commission by making disciples of all nations. Help us to seize the amazing opportunities for evangelism that You place all around us. Show me how I can join my brothers and sisters in Christ in using my time, talent, and treasure wisely and with a sense of urgency to reach the lost and build up Your church. In Jesus' name I pray. Amen.

★ ★ ★

Go therefore and make disciples of all the nations,
baptizing them in the name of the Father and the Son
and the Holy Spirit, teaching them to observe all that
I commanded you; and lo, I am with you always,
even to the end of the age.

—MATTHEW 28:19–20

Acknowledgments

No single person can be credited with the creation of the United States of America. George Washington might be considered the father of our nation, but he was not alone in fighting the revolution for independence or in molding thirteen separate colonies into a unified whole. The birth of our beloved country required a dedicated group of people, whom we call founding fathers and founding mothers.

Creating a book is not the same as creating a country, though they do share one thing in common: the commitment of more than one person. My name may appear on the cover of this book, but it really belongs to the team that makes my ministry possible. To them, I am deeply indebted.

Jeana Ledbetter and her gifted team at Hachette Book Group immediately caught the vision of this book. They ensured that the final product was accurate, readable, and beautiful.

Joe Sneed, whose careful attention to historical detail and precise theological and biblical knowledge kept this book historically correct and biblically rich.

Jennifer Stair, who used her literary skills to assist me in sharpening mine, made sure that each sentence and paragraph was a joy to read.

Sealy Yates, my literary agent and trusted advisor for more years than I wish to count, found just the right home for publishing this book.

Carrilyn Baker, the finest executive assistant any pastor could ever hope to work with, has juggled my schedule and kept me on track and done so with humility and grace rarely seen these days.

Notes

★ ★ ★

Introduction: America's Only Hope

1. Abraham Lincoln, "The National Fast: Proclamation by the President of the United States," April 30, 1863, *New York Times*, http://www.nytimes.com/1863/04/30/archives/the-national-fast-proclamation-by-the-president-of-the-united.html.

2. Abraham Lincoln, "Second Annual Message to Congress," US National Archives and Records Administration, December 1, 1862, http://www.archives.gov/legislative/features/sotu/lincoln.html.

1. For God's Will to Be Done

1. Susie Federer, *Miracles in American History: 32 Amazing Stories of Answered Prayer* (St. Louis: Amerisearch, 2014), 83–85.

2. George Washington, "To John Adams, President of the United States," July 13, 1798, as quoted in *The Writings of George Washington*, vol. 11, ed. Jared Sparks (Boston: Little, Brown, and Company, 1855), 262.

3. John Adams, "Proclamation for a National Fast," March 6, 1799, in John Adams, *The Works of John Adams: Letters and State Papers, 1799–1811*, vol. 9, ed. Charles Francis Adams (Boston: Little, Brown, and Company, 1854), 173.

4. Robert Jeffress, "How a Christian Should Vote, Part One" sermon, First Baptist Church of Dallas, Texas, October 16, 2011.

5. Jeffress, "How a Christian Should Vote."

2. For Religious Freedom

1. Facts for this chapter were found in the following sources: William Bradford, *Of Plymouth Plantation, A New Edition; The Complete Text with Notes and an Introduction by Samuel Eliot Morison* (New York: Alfred A. Knopf, 2002), xii, 23–45; William Bradford, *Bradford's History of the Plymouth Settlement, 1608–1650*, trans. Harold Paget (New York: E. P. Dutton & Company, 1920), 21, 63–89; William Bradford, "The Pilgrim Press in Choir Alley, Leyden; And Its Suppression; Together with the Books That Were Produced By It, Between October 1616 and June 1619," *The Story of the Pilgrim Fathers, 1606–1623 A.D.; as told by Themselves, their Friends, and their Enemies*, ed. Edward Arber (London: Ward and Downey Limited, 1897), 195–197; Michael Medved, *The American Miracle* (New York: Crown Forum, 2016), 30–46; Mary B. Sherwood, *Pilgrim: A Biography of William Brewster* (Falls Church, VA: Great Oak Press of Virginia, 1982), 117; Bradford Smith, *Bradford of Plymouth* (Philadelphia: J. B. Lippincott, 1951), 78.

2. Parts of this paragraph are adapted from Robert Jeffress, *Twilight's Last Gleaming* (Franklin, TN: Worthy, 2016), 218–232.

3. For Truth to Prevail

1. Adam Candeub and Mark Epstein, "Platform, or Publisher?," *City Journal*, May 7, 2018, Manhattan Institute for Policy Research, http://www.city-journal.org/html/platform-or-publisher-15888.html.

2. Alex Hern, "How Alphabet Became the Biggest Company in the World," *The Guardian*, February 2, 2016, http://www.theguardian.com/technology/2016/feb/01/how-alphabet-made-google-biggest-company-in-the-world.

3. Statistics are true at the time of writing. Stacy Fisher, "The Top 10 Most Popular Sites of 2020," Lifewire, last modified January 2, 2020, http://www.lifewire.com/most-popular-sites-3483140.

4. Statistics are true at the time of writing. Craig Smith, "365 Interesting Google Search Statistics and Much More (2020): By the Numbers," last modified February 9, 2020, http://expandedramblings.com/index.php/by-the-numbers-a-gigantic-list-of-google-stats-and-facts; Jillian D'Onfro, "More than 70% of Internet Traffic during Peak Hours Now Comes from Video and Music Streaming," Business Insider, December 7, 2015, http://www.businessinsider.com/sandvine-bandwidth-data-shows-70-of-internet-traffic-is-video-and-music-streaming-2015-12.

5. "Current Sr. Google Engineer Goes Public on Camera: Tech Is 'Dangerous,' 'Taking Sides,'" Project Veritas, July 24, 2019, http://www.projectveritas.com/2019/07/24/current-sr-google-engineer-goes-public-on-camera-tech-is-dangerous-taking-sides; Rachel Stoltzfoos, "19 Insane Tidbits from James Damore's Lawsuit about Google's Office Environment," The Federalist, January 10, 2018, http://thefederalist.com/2018/01/10/19-insane-tidbits-james-damores-lawsuit-googles-office-environment; James Damore, "What Happens When Google Disagrees with You?," Prager University video, November 8, 2017, http://www.prageru.com/video/what-happens-when-google-disagrees-with-you.

6. Will Knight, "Biased Algorithms Are Everywhere, and No One Seems to Care," *MIT Technology Review*, July 12, 2017, accessed September 13, 2019, http://www.technologyreview.com/s/608248/biased-algorithms-are-everywhere-and-no-one-seems-to-care; Robert Epstein and Ronald E. Robertson, "The Search Engine Manipulation Effect (SEME) and Its Possible Impact on the Outcomes of Elections," *Proceedings of the National Academy of Sciences of the United States of America* 112, no. 33 (August 18, 2015): E4512–E4521, http://www.pnas.org/content/pnas/112/33/E4512.full.pdf.

7. Eric Lieberman, "Google's New Fact-Check Feature Almost Exclusively Targets Conservative Sites," Daily Caller News Foundation, January 9, 2018, http://dailycaller.com/2018/01/09/googles-new-fact-check-feature-almost-exclusively-targets-conservative-sites; Mark Hodges, "Google's New Fact-Check Operates Just Like Orwell's 1984 'Ministry of Truth,'" Life Site News, January 12, 2018, http://www.lifesitenews.com/blogs/googles-new-fact-check-operates-just-like-orwells-1984-ministry-of-truth.

8. Type in any two phrases and you can see the relative number of people searching for those phrases over time. For example: https://trends.google.com/trends/explore?geo=US&q=men%20can%20cook,women%20can%20cook.

9. "Current Sr. Google Engineer Goes Public"; "Project Veritas Re-Uploads Google Exposé Taken Down by YouTube ahead of White House Social Media Summit," July 11, 2019, http://www.projectveritas.com/2019/07/11/project-veritas-re-uploads-google-expose-taken-down-by-youtube-ahead-of-white-house-social-media-summit; official internal Google documents leaked to Project Veritas, http://www.projectveritas.com/google-document-dump; Robert Epstein, interview with Mark Levin, *Life, Liberty, and Levin*, Fox News Corporation, September 6, 2019, http://video.foxnews.com/v/6084154651001/#sp=show-clips.

10. "Demonetized" means that they take away the ability for that video to make any

money for its creators. "Shadow banned" means that the video does not appear in the suggestion area to the right of the video playing.

11. Brent Bozell, "Big Tech Is Big Brother," Prager University, June 3, 2019, http://www .prageru.com/video/big-tech-is-big-brother.

12. "New Google Document Leaked Describing Shapiro, Prager, as 'Nazis Using the Dogwhistles,'" Project Veritas, June 25, 2109, http://www.projectveritas.com/2019/06 /25/breaking-new-google-document-leaked-describing-shapiro-prager-as-nazis-using -the-dogwhistles; John Gage, "Crenshaw Calls Google 'Disturbing' after Employee Calls Ben Shapiro a 'Nazi,'" *Washington Examiner*, June 26, 2019, http://www .washingtonexaminer.com/news/crenshaw-calls-google-disturbing-after-employee -calls-ben-shapiro-a-nazi.

13. David French, "Google's Discrimination against Conservatives Is Just the Beginning for Corporate America," *Dallas Morning News*, January 11, 2018, http://www.dallasnews .com/opinion/commentary/2018/01/11/google-s-discrimination-against-conservatives -is-just-the-beginning-for-corporate-america.

14. Dennis Prager, "Dennis Prager Testifies before the U.S. Senate on Big Tech Censorship," testimony before Congress on July 16, 2019, http://www.youtube.com/watch?v =llt6kiwKwVI; Eric George, "PragerU v. YouTube," Prager University, August 19, 2019, accessed September 3, 2019, http://www.prageru.com/video/prageru-v-youtube.

15. Jen Gennai openly admits this in an undercover recording. Zach Vorhies and Greg Coppola relay this information in interviews on Project Veritas; "Project Veritas Re-Uploads Google Exposé"; "Google 'Machine Learning Fairness' Whistleblower Goes Public, Says: 'Burden Lifted off of My Soul,'" August 14, 2019, http://www .projectveritas.com/2019/08/14/google-machine-learning-fairness-whistleblower-goes -public-says-burden-lifted-off-of-my-soul.

16. Robert Epstein, testimony before Congress on July 16, 2019, found at American Institute for Behavioral Research and Technology, "Why Google Poses a Serious Threat to Democracy, and How to End That Threat," June 16, 2019, http://www .judiciary.senate.gov/imo/media/doc/Epstein%20Testimony.pdf; "User Clip: Dr. Robert Epstein Testimony," July 18, 2019, http://www.c-span.org/video/?c4808451 /dr-robert-epstein-testimony; Robert Epstein, interview with Tucker Carlson, *Tucker Carlson Tonight*, Fox News, March 23, 2018, http://www.youtube.com/watch?v =FAfOv9VHnTs; Robert Epstein, interview with Evan Halper, "This Psychologist Claims Google Search Results Unfairly Steer Voters to the Left. Conservatives Love Him," *Los Angeles Times*, March 22, 2019, http://www.latimes.com/politics/la-na-pol -google-search-bias-elections-20190322-story.html; Robert Epstein, interview with Mark Levin, "Dr. Robert Epstein on Google's Ability to Affect the Outcome of Elections," Fox News, September 9, 2019, http://video.foxnews.com/v/6084521411001; Epstein and Robertson, "The Search Engine Manipulation Effect."

17. Dennis Prager, testifying before Congress on July 16, 2019, "Dennis Prager Testifies before the U.S. Senate on Big Tech Censorship," July 17, 2019, accessed September 3, 2019, http://www.youtube.com/watch?v=llt6kiwKwVI.

4. For Protection from Our Enemies

1. Pearl Harbor Visitors Bureau, "How Many People Died at Pearl Harbor during the Attack?," accessed January 15, 2020, http://visitpearlharbor.org/faqs/how-many-people -died-at-pearl-harbor-during-the-attack; "Pearl Harbor," History.com, updated December 6, 2019, http://www.history.com/topics/world-war-ii/pearl-harbor; Akira

Iriye, interview with Laurence Rees, "Mentality of the Japanese," WW2History (personal website for scholarly research), accessed January 10, 2020, http://ww2history .com/experts/Akira_Iriye/Mentality_of_the_Japanese; Walter A. Skya, *Japan's Holy War: The Ideology of Radical Shinto Ultranationalism* (Durham, NC: Duke University Press, 2009), 195–198, 269–270, 326–328.

2. "September 11 Attacks," History.com, updated September 11, 2019, http://www .history.com/topics/21st-century/9-11-attacks; Roy Speckhardt, "9/11 Attackers Used Religion Just As ISIS Does Today," HuffPost, updated September 10, 2017, http:// www.huffpost.com/entry/september-11-attackers-us_b_11937950.

3. John Philip Jenkins, "Oklahoma City Bombing," *Encyclopaedia Britannica*, last updated November 1, 2019, http://www.britannica.com/event/Oklahoma-City-bombing; Official FBI historical account, "Oklahoma City Bombing," Federal Bureau of Investigation, accessed January 15, 2020, http://www.fbi.gov/history/famous-cases /oklahoma-city-bombing; FBI commemorative supplement, "The Oklahoma City Bombing: 20 Years Later," Federal Bureau of Investigation, accessed January 10, 2020, http://stories.fbi.gov/oklahoma-bombing.

5. For National Unity

1. Facts for this chapter were found in the following sources: Brian Dunbar, "Apollo 8: Christmas at the Moon," NASA, updated December 26, 2019, http://www.nasa.gov /topics/history/features/apollo_8.html; Matthew Twombly and Kendrick McDonald, "A Timeline of 1968: The Year That Shattered America," *Smithsonian Magazine*, January 2018, http://www.smithsonianmag.com/history/timeline-seismic-180967503; "1968 Events," History.com, last updated August 21, 2018, http://www.history.com /topics/1960s/1968-events; "The Space Race," History.com, updated November 14, 2019, http://www.history.com/topics/cold-war/space-race; Erin Blakemore, "Buzz Aldrin Took Holy Communion on the Moon. NASA Kept It Quiet," History.com, updated September 6, 2019, http://www.history.com/news/buzz-aldrin-communion -apollo-11-nasa.

6. For Fair Elections

1. Facts for this chapter were found in the following sources: Martin Tolchin, "How Johnson Won Election He'd Lost," *New York Times*, February 11, 1990, http://www. nytimes.com/1990/02/11/us/how-johnson-won-election-he-d-lost.html; Dan Balz, "The Mystery of Ballot Box 13," *Washington Post*, March 4, 1990, http://www .washingtonpost.com/archive/entertainment/books/1990/03/04/the-mystery-of-ballot -box-13/70206359-8543-48e3-9ce2-f3c4fdf6da3d; John Gibbs, "Voter Fraud Is Real. Here's the Proof," The Federalist, October 13, 2016, http://thefederalist.com/2016 /10/13/voter-fraud-real-heres-proof; "Heritage Explains Voter Fraud," Heritage Foundation, accessed January 15, 2020, http://www.heritage.org/election-integrity /heritage-explains/voter-fraud; "Election Fraud Cases from across the United States," Heritage Foundation, accessed January 10, 2020, http://www.heritage.org/voterfraud; Tom Fitton, "Tom Fitton Estimates 900,000 Illegal Votes by Aliens in Midterm Elections!," February 8, 2019, http://www.youtube.com/watch/?v=d30vKLd9CXQ; Robert McNamara, "Tammany Hall," ThoughtCo., updated April 5, 2019, http:// www.thoughtco.com/history-of-tammany-hall-1774023; "Ex-Official Says He Stole 1948 Election for Johnson," *New York Times*, July 31, 1977, http://www.nytimes.com /1977/07/31/archives/exofficial-says-he-stole-1948-election-for-johnson-most -involved.html.

7. For Our President and Leaders in Washington

1. Many facts for this chapter were found in the following sources: Mark Bowden, "'Idiot,' 'Yahoo,' 'Original Gorilla': How Lincoln Was Dissed in His Day," *The Atlantic*, June 2013, http://www.theatlantic.com/magazine/archive/2013/06/abraham-lincoln -is-an-idiot/309304; "Abraham Lincoln," History.com, updated January 17, 2020, http:// www.history.com/topics/us-presidents/abraham-lincoln (italics in original).

2. Parts of this prayer come from Robert Jeffress's prayer for President Trump and our nation in the Oval Office on September 1, 2017, and from a prayer he gave at a campaign rally in Dallas, Texas, on September 16, 2015. Text for prayers found at "Dr. Jeffress and President Trump Call for Nation to Pray," First Baptist Dallas, September 1, 2017, http://www .firstdallas.org/news/dr-jeffress-and-president-trump-call-for-nation-to-pray; and Bob Allen, "Robert Jeffress Prays 'Special Blessing' on Donald Trump," Baptist News, September 16, 2015, http://baptistnews.com/article/robert-jeffress-prays-special-blessing -on-donald-trump.

8. For Our State and Local Leaders

1. Matthew Spalding, "The Man Who Would Not Be King," Heritage Foundation, February 5, 2007, http://www.heritage.org/commentary/the-man-who-would-not-be -king; Other facts for this section are from Michael Hattem, "Newburgh Conspiracy," Fred W. Smith National Library for the Study of George Washington at Mount Vernon, George Washington Library, accessed June 18, 2019, http://www .mountvernon.org/library/digitalhistory/digital-encyclopedia/article/newburgh -conspiracy; Ron Chernow, *Washington: A Life* (New York: Penguin, 2010), 434–436.

2. David Boaz, "The Man Who Would Not Be King," Cato Institute, February 20, 2006, http://www.cato.org/publications/commentary/man-who-would-not-be-king.

3. Some facts for this chapter were found in the following sources: Ron Chernow, "George Washington: The Reluctant President," *Smithsonian Magazine*, February 2011, http:// www.smithsonianmag.com/history/george-washington-the-reluctant-president-49492; Spalding, "The Man Who Would Not Be King"; "What Is a Constitutional Democratic Republic?," Reference.com, accessed June 17, 2019, http://www.reference.com/government -politics/constitutional-democratic-republic-94535bfb08c336da.

9. For Christians to Answer God's Call to Lead

1. Mike Huckabee, interview at the Kennedy School of Government: Institute of Politics at Harvard University, "A Conversation with Mike Huckabee: Institute of Politics," April 23, 2014, 28:00–28:40, http://www.youtube.com/watch?v=kMXJW2bRzLE.

2. "I Don't (Heart) Huckabee," *Seattle Times*, December 14, 2007, http://www .seattletimes.com/opinion/i-dont-heart-huckabee; "16 Things to Know about…Mike Huckabee," PBS, November 10, 2015, http://www.pbs.org/weta/washingtonweek /blog-post/16-things-know-about-mike-huckabee.

3. Mike Huckabee, *From Hope to Higher Ground* (New York: Hachette Book Group, 2007), 7.

4. Huckabee, interview, April 23, 2014, 5:30–6:00.

5. Huckabee, *From Hope to Higher Ground*, 6–7.

6. Some facts for this chapter were found in the following sources: "Mike Huckabee," *Encyclopaedia Britannica*, accessed January 15, 2020, http://www.britannica.com /biography/Mike-Huckabee; Jodi Kantor and David D. Kirkpatrick, "Ministry Was Springboard for Huckabee's Political Career," *New York Times*, December 6, 2017, http:// www.nytimes.com/2007/12/06/world/americas/06iht-huckabee.1.8612028

.html; Huckabee, interview, April 23, 2014; Huckabee, *From Hope to Higher Ground.*

7. Mike Huckabee, interview, April 23, 2014, 11:38–12:06.

8. Constitutional Convention Delegates, Preamble to the Constitution of the United States of America (Philadelphia: Constitutional Convention, 1787), accessed January 11, 2020, http://www.whitehouse.gov/about-the-white-house/the-constitution. See also the first and second paragraphs of the Declaration of Independence, National Archives, http://www.archives.gov/founding-docs/declaration-transcript. See also *The Constitution of the United States of America with the Declaration of Independence* (New York: Fall River Press, 2012), 37, 81–82.

9. Wayne Grudem, *Politics According to the Bible* (Grand Rapids, MI: Zondervan, 2010), 61–62.

10. For Righteous Judges and Justices

1. Some facts for this chapter were found in the following sources: "14th Amendment," History.com, updated August 21, 2018, http://www.history.com/topics/black-history/fourteenth-amendment; "Dred Scott Decision," History.com, updated July 27, 2019, accessed January 10, 2020, http://www.history.com/this-day-in-history/dred-scott-decision.

2. Some facts for this chapter were found in the following sources: Chief Justice Roger B. Taney, "The Dred Scott Decision: Opinion of Chief Justice Taney," Library of Congress, accessed May 23, 2019, http://www.loc.gov/item/17001543; "Dred Scott Case," History.com, accessed January 10, 2020, http://www.history.com/topics/black-history/dred-scott-case.

3. Parts of this section adapted from Robert Jeffress, "How a Christian Should Vote, Part One," sermon, October 16, 2011, First Baptist Church of Dallas, Texas, and Robert Jeffress, "How a Christian Should Vote, Part Two," sermon, October 23, 2011, First Baptist Church of Dallas, Texas.

11. For Our Troops

1. Continental Congress, "Congressional Fast Day Proclamation," March 16, 1776, Library of Congress, http://www.loc.gov/exhibits/religion/rel04.html#obj107.

2. Federer, *Miracles in American History: 32 Amazing Stories of Answered Prayer*, 46.

3. "Battle of Long Island" (video), History.com, updated August 21, 2018, http://www.history.com/topics/american-revolution/battle-of-long-island.

4. Found at http://totallyhistory.com/battle-of-long-island on May 15, 2019.

5. Many facts for this chapter were found in Federer, *Miracles in American History*, 45–48.

12. For Law Enforcement

1. Facts for this chapter were found in the following sources: "Bass Reeves; American Lawman," *Encyclopaedia Britannica*, last updated January 8, 2020, http://www.britannica.com/biography/Bass-Reeves; Thad Morgan, "Was the Real Lone Ranger a Black Man?," History.com, updated August 31, 2018, http://www.history.com/news/bass-reeves-real-lone-ranger-a-black-man; Art T. Burton, "Bass Reeves," National Park Service, US Department of the Interior, updated April 10, 2015, http://www.nps.gov/fosm/learn/historyculture/bass_reeves.htm.

2. For instance, see 1 Peter 2:13–17.

3. See also Genesis 9:6 for when God first gave this mandate.

4. See also Exodus 1:15–21 and Daniel 6:11–23.

13. For First Responders

1. "September 11 Attacks," History.com, last updated September 11, 2019, http://www
.history.com/topics/21st-century/9-11-attacks.

2. Some facts for this chapter were found in the following sources: "September 11
Attacks," History.com; Inae Oh and Nick Wing, "16 Sobering Numbers That Remind
Us to Honor the Sacrifice of 9/11 Responders," HuffPost, updated December 6, 2017,
http://www.huffpost.com/entry/911-first-responders_n_5797398; National Fallen
Firefighters Foundation, "Roll of Honor: William M. Feehan," accessed July 19, 2019,
http://www.firehero.org/fallen-firefighter/william-m-feehan; "9/11 Memorial and
Museum," National September 11 Memorial & Museum, accessed July 19, 2019,
http://www.911memorial.org.

14. For Our Debt Problems

1. Interviews with Ivor van Heerden on October 29, 2004; September 10, 2005; and
October 5, 2005, "The Man Who Predicted Katrina," *Nova*, Public Broadcasting
Service, November 21, 2005, http://www.pbs.org/wgbh/nova/article/predicting
-katrina.

2. More facts for this chapter were found in the following sources: Douglas Brinkley,
"The Broken Promise of the Levees That Failed New Orleans," *Smithsonian Magazine*,
September 2015, http://www.smithsonianmag.com/smithsonian-institution/broken
-promise-levees-failed-new-orleans-180956326; "Hurricane Katrina," History.com,
updated August 9, 2019, http://www.history.com/topics/natural-disasters-and
-environment/hurricane-katrina; Lindsey Cook and Ethan Rosenberg, "No One Knows
How Many People Died in Katrina," *U.S. News & World Report*, August 28, 2015,
http://www.usnews.com/news/blogs/data-mine/2015/08/28/no-one-knows-how-many
-people-died-in-katrina; Pierre Thomas, "Exclusive: Were the Warning Signs of Katrina
Ignored?," ABC News, September 12, 2005, http://abcnews.go.com/GMA
/HurricaneKatrina/exclusive-warning-signs-katrina/story?id=1117497; Richard A.
Serrano and Nicole Gaouette, "Despite Warnings, Washington Failed to Fund Levee
Projects," *Los Angeles Times*, September 4, 2005, http://www.latimes.com/archives
/la-xpm-2005-sep-04-na-levee4-story.html; Matt Mayer, Diem Salmon, and Richard
Weitz, "The Local Role in Disaster Response: Lessons from Katrina and the California
Wildfires," Heritage Foundation, June 4, 2008, http://www.heritage.org/defense/report
/the-local-role-disaster-response-lessons-katrina-and-the-california-wildfires; Mayra
Rodriguez Valladares, "America's Largest Cities Are Practically Broke," *Forbes*, January
29, 2019, http://www.forbes.com/sites/mayrarodriguezvalladares/2019/01/29/americas
-largest-cities-are-practically-broke/#207f268e2ebb; Jordan J. Ballor, "America's Public
Debt: Crisis or the Cost of Civilization?," Acton Institute, February 6, 2019, http://
acton.org/pub/commentary/2019/02/06/americas-public-debt-crisis-or-cost
-civilization; Congressional Budget Office, "The Budget and Economic Outlook:
2019 to 2029," Congress of the United States, January 2019, https://www.cbo.gov
/system/files/2019-03/54918-Outlook-3.pdf; Jessica Dickler, "Consumer Debt Hits
$4 Trillion," CNBC, updated February 21, 2019, http://www.cnbc.com/2019/02/21
/consumer-debt-hits-4-trillion.html; Zack Friedman, "Student Loan Debt Statistics In
2019: A $1.5 Trillion Crisis," *Forbes*, February 25, 2019, http://www.forbes.com/sites
/zackfriedman/2019/02/25/student-loan-debt-statistics-2019/#57bc0553133f; Brian
Riedl, "Getting to Yes: A History of Why Budget Negotiations Succeed, and Why
They Fail," Manhattan Institute, June 18, 2019, http://www.manhattan-institute.org
/three-ingredients-successful-deficit-reduction-federal-budget.

3. Adapted from Robert Jeffress, *Second Chance, Second Act; Study Guide* (Dallas: Pathway to Victory, 2017), 20.

4. Winston Churchill, "Town Hall, Malmesbury, 18 December 1904," *Complete Speeches* 1: 398, http://richardlangworth.com/taxprosperity.

5. For more information about Financial Peace University, see http://www.daveramsey.com/fpu.

15. For Education

1. Facts for this chapter were found in the following sources: Jack Lynch, "Every Man Able to Read," *CW Journal* (winter 2011), Colonial Williamsburg Foundation, http://www.history.org/Foundation/journal/Winter11/literacy.cfm; "A Brief History of Literacy," University of Texas at Arlington, September 9, 2015, http://academicpartnerships.uta.edu/articles/education/brief-history-of-literacy.aspx; John L. Puckett, "Literacy in the Colonial Period," from the course American Education Reform: History, Policy, Practice, University of Pennsylvania, accessed August 9, 2019, http://www.coursera.org/lecture/edref/1-3-literacy-in-the-colonial-period-CEKxg.

2. The Westminster Divines, *The Westminster Shorter Catechism* (London: Westminster Assembly, 1647), http://westminsterconfession.org/confessional-standards/the-westminster-shorter-catechism.php.

3. Robert Jeffress, "Success without Succession Is Failure," sermon, May 12, 2013, First Baptist Church of Dallas, Texas.

16. For Pure Sexuality

1. Robert Jeffress, "Secret #5: Graze in Your Own Pasture," *The Solomon Secrets* (Dallas: Pathway to Victory, 2013).

2. Facts for this chapter were found in the following sources: "Why Is the Liberty Bell Cracked?," History.com, updated August 31, 2018, http://www.history.com/news/why-is-the-liberty-bell-cracked; "Inscription on the Liberty Bell," Museum of the Bible, accessed January 15, 2020, http://www.museumofthebible.org/book/minutes/644; "The Liberty Bell," National Park Service, US Department of the Interior, updated March 16, 2019, http://www.nps.gov/inde/learn/historyculture/stories-libertybell.htm.

17. For Godly Marriages

1. Some facts for this chapter were found in the following sources: Billy Graham Evangelistic Association, "Footprints of a Pilgrim—Remembering Ruth Bell Graham (Full Program)," November 8, 2016, http://www.youtube.com/watch?v=is9MrevpN88; "Billy Graham Dies: His Tribute to His Wife, Ruth," Citizen Times, updated February 21, 2018, accessed January 15, 2020, http://www.citizen-times.com/story/news/local/2018/02/21/billys-tribute-wife-ruth/110665632; "Billy Graham," Biography.com, updated April 17, 2019, http://www.biography.com/religious-figure/billy-graham; Kristen Driscoll, Amanda Knoke, Jerri Menges, and Bob Paulson, "Ruth Bell Graham: A Life Well Lived," *Decision*, July 24, 2007, http://billygraham.org/decision-magazine/june-2013/ruth-bell-graham-a-life-well-lived; Randall Balmer, "Billy Graham: American Evangelist," *Encyclopaedia Britannica*, last updated January 1, 2020, http://www.britannica.com/biography/Billy-Graham.

2. Adapted from Robert Jeffress, "What Every Woman Wants…What Every Man Needs," sermon, April 19, 2009, First Baptist Church of Dallas, Texas.

3. Billy Graham, "Answers," Billy Graham Evangelistic Association, April 8, 2016, http://billygraham.org/answer/newlyweds-should-make-christ-the-foundation-of-marriage.

4. Adapted from Robert Jeffress, "Say Goodbye to Marital Regrets," sermon, June 21, 1998, First Baptist Church of Wichita Falls, Texas.

18. For the Voiceless

1. Gianna Jessen, from an interview with a member of my staff on August 24, 2018. Unless otherwise noted, all quotations and details about Jessen's story come from this interview.
2. "Number of Abortions—Abortion Counters," self-updating count, Life Matters, accessed April 10, 2019, http://www.numberofabortions.com. Numbers based on statistics and trends documented and cataloged on http://www.lifematterstv.org/abortioncounters.html on April 10, 2019.
3. Lila Rose, "The Human Rights Abuses of the Abortion Industry Must End," Live Action, accessed April 10, 2019, http://www.liveaction.org.
4. "Oral Contraceptives and Abortion," Texas Right to Life, July 20, 2010, http://www.texasrighttolife.com/oral-contraceptives-and-abortion.
5. Adapted from Robert Jeffress, *Twilight's Last Gleaming* (Brentwood, TN: Worthy, 2011).
6. "How Early Can an Ultrasound Detect a Heartbeat?," Zocdoc.com, accessed April 10, 2019, http://www.zocdoc.com/answers/3816/how-early-can-an-ultrasound-detect-a-heartbeat.
7. Michelle Lawson, "Child Development Stages in the Womb," Healthfully, June 13, 2017, http://healthfully.com/261812-child-development-stages-in-the-womb.html; Brian J. Stillwell, *The Biology of Prenatal Development* (Manchester, NH: Endowment for Human Development, 2006), 11–12, http://www.ehd.org/pdf/BPD%204-26-2006%20English.pdf.
8. Robin Pierucci, "Neonatologist: Babies Do Feel Pain in the Womb. I've Seen It," The Federalist, January 29, 2018, http://thefederalist.com/2018/01/29/neonatologist-babies-feel-pain-womb-ive-seen.

19. For the Crisis of Fatherless Children

1. "Family & His Youth," Father Flanagan League, accessed August 20, 2019, http://fatherflanagan.org/biography.
2. "His Work & Mission," Father Flanagan League, accessed August 20, 2019, http://fatherflanagan.org/biography.
3. "Father Edward J. Flanagan," Boys Town, accessed August 20, 2019, http://www.boystown.org/about/father-flanagan/Pages/default.aspx.
4. Other facts for this chapter were found in the following sources: Boys Town information pages, accessed August 18, 2019, http://www.boystown.org/about/father-flanagan/Pages/default.aspx, http://www.boystown.org/100/timeline/Pages/default.aspx, http://www.boystown.org/about/father-flanagan/Pages/flanagan-timeline.aspx, http://www.boystown.org/about/father-flanagan/Pages/father-flanagan-quotes.aspx, and http://www.boystown.org/100/get-involved/Pages/americas-number-one-war-dad.aspx; Chloe Langr "Father Flanagan, the Founder of Boys Town, Is One Step Closer to Sainthood," Epic Pew, accessed August 18, 2019, http://epicpew.com/flanagan-boys-town-canonization.
5. Wayne Parker, "Statistics on Fatherless Children in America," LiveAbout.com, updated May 24, 2019, http://www.liveabout.com/fatherless-children-in-america-statistics-1270392.
6. Jeffress, *Twilight's Last Gleaming*, 67–68.
7. Mark Meckler, "Of 27 Deadliest Mas Shooters, 26 of Them Had One Thing in Common," Patheos, February 20, 2018, accessed August 20, 2019, http://www

.patheos.com/blogs/markmeckler/2018/02/27-deadliest-mass-shooters-26-one-thing
-common.

20. For Those in Prison

1. Jack Murphy, interview with staff writer, "Murf the Surf: He Stole the Star of India, Killed Two Women in the Whiskey Creek Murders, but That's Not Him Any More," *Tampa Bay Times*, September 1, 2012, http://www.tampabay.com/features /humaninterest/murf-the-surf-he-stole-the-star-of-india-killed-two-women-in-the -whiskey/1247688.
2. Murphy, "Murf the Surf."
3. Jack Murphy, interview at Christian Family Outreach Center, "Jack Murphy (Murph the Surf)," October 26, 2012, http://www.youtube.com/watch?v=r7fxvwBg0K4. All other facts about Jack Murphy were found in the following sources: Murphy, "Murf the Surf,"; Murphy, interview at Christian Family Outreach Center; Tim Eberly, "Infamous Jewel Thief Murf the Surf Recalls Time in Virginia Beach," *Virginia Pilot*, June 7, 2018, 2019, http://www.pilotonline.com/ask/article_a9ec6a8a-6057-11e8-8327-0725aa894da0.html; David Sears, "How Three Amateur Jewel Thieves Made Off with New York's Most Precious Gems," *Smithsonian Magazine*, February 25, 2014, http:// www.smithsonianmag.com/history/how-three-amateur-jewel-thieves-made-new-yorks -most-precious-gems-180949885.
4. "Why Help Prisoners?," Prison Fellowship, infographic, accessed September 5, 2019, http://www.prisonfellowship.org/why-help-prisoners.
5. "Why Help Prisoners?"

21. For the Hurting

1. Anna Spafford, "Anna's Telegram to Horatio," American Colony Museum, Library of Congress, December 1871, http://www.loc.gov/exhibits/americancolony/amcolony -family.html#obj6.
2. Horatio Spafford, personal letter to a relative, "The American Colony in Jerusalem," Library of Congress, December 1871, http://www.loc.gov/exhibits/americancolony /amcolony-family.html#obj8.
3. Pastor Weiss, Spafford Family Album, "The American Colony in Jerusalem," December 1871, Library of Congress, http://www.loc.gov/exhibits/americancolony/amcolony -family.html#obj1.
4. Other facts for this chapter were found in the following sources: Thomas E. Corts, *Seeking Solace: The Life and Legacy of Horatio G. Spafford* (Birmingham, AL: Samford University Press, 2013); Rachael Phillips, *Well with My Soul: Four Dramatic Stories of Great Hymn Writers* (Uhrichsville, OH: Barbour, 2004); Horatio Spafford, "The American Colony in Jerusalem," Library of Congress, December 1871, http://www .loc.gov/exhibits/americancolony/amcolony-family.html; Online Exhibit, "Horatio Spafford," Friends of Zion Museum, accessed September 9, 2019, http://www .fozmuseum.com/explore-foz/horatio-spafford.

22. To Know History and Learn from It

1. George Santayana, *The Life of Reason, Volume 1. Reason in Common Sense* (New York: Charles Scribner's Sons, 1905), 284.
2. Facts for this chapter were found in the following sources: Stephen L. Hardin, *Texian Iliad: A Military History of the Texas Revolution* (Austin: University of Texas Press,

1996); T. R. Fehrenbach, *Lone Star: A History of Texas and the Texans* (Boston: Da Capo Press, 2000); The Alamo Trust, "The Alamo Chronology," The Alamo, accessed May 9, 2019, http://thealamo.org/remember/history/chronology/index.html; "Texas Declares Independence," History.com, updated July 27, 2019, http://www.history.com /this-day-in-history/texas-declares-independence; Jeff Wallenfeldt, "Texas Revolution," *Encyclopaedia Britannica*, last updated December 15, 2017, http://www.britannica .com/topic/Texas-Revolution/Santa-Anna-responds-the-Alamo-and-the-Goliad -Massacre.

23. For Fellow Christians Who Are "Completely Wrong"

1. Interview with Kirsten Powers, "Fox News' Highly Reluctant Jesus Follower," *Christianity Today*, October 22, 2013, http://www.christianitytoday.com/ct/2013 /november/fox-news-highly-reluctant-jesus-follower-kirsten-powers.html.
2. Robert Jeffress, "The Scarlet Harlot," sermon, March 7, 2010, First Baptist Church of Dallas, Texas.

24. To Seize Opportunities God Gives Us

1. Facts for this chapter were found in the following sources: A'Lelia Bundles, *On Her Own Ground: The Life and Times of Madam C. J. Walker* (New York: Washington Square Press, 2001); "Madam C. J. Walker," History.com, last updated August 21, 2018, http://www.history.com/topics/black-history/madame-c-j-walker; A'Lelia Bundles, "Madam C. J. Walker," *Encyclopaedia Britannica*, last updated December 19, 2019, http://www.britannica.com/biography/Madam-C-J-Walker. In this entry, Bundles describes Madam Walker as "one of the first African American female millionaires in the United States." However, in her biography of Walker, Bundles admits that she certainly was not a millionaire at the time of her passing.

25. To Do Our Jobs as for Jesus

1. Facts for this chapter were found in the following sources: Mary Bagley, "George Washington Carver: Biography, Inventions & Quotes," LiveScience, December 7, 2013, http://www.livescience.com/41780-george-washington-carver.html; William J. Federer, *George Washington Carver: His Life & Faith In His Own Words* (St. Louis: Amerisearch, 2002); George Washington Carver, *George Washington Carver in His Own Words*, ed. Gary R. Kremer (Columbia: University of Missouri Press, 1991).
2. Robert Jeffress, "Forgotten, Forsaken, Forever?" sermon, January 25, 2009, First Baptist Church of Dallas, Texas.

26. For Christians to Produce Godly Art with Excellence

1. Some facts for this chapter were found in the following sources: Joy Allmond, "Johnny Cash's Faith and Friendship with Billy Graham," Billy Graham Evangelistic Association, September 13, 2015, http://billygraham.org/story/johnny-cashs-faith-and-friendship -with-billy-graham; Greg Laurie with Marshall Terrill, *Johnny Cash: The Redemption of an American Icon* (Washington, DC: Regnery, 2019); Johnny Cash, *Man in Black* (Grand Rapids, MI: Chosen Books, 1985).
2. See Acts 2:1–18 and Romans 8:9.
3. See Proverbs 22:29, 1 Peter 4:10–11, Daniel 1:17, and 2 Timothy 1:6–7.
4. See Matthew 25:14–30 and Romans 12:6–8.

27. For Gratitude

1. Some facts for this chapter were found in the following sources: Drew Gilpin Faust, *This Republic of Suffering: Death and the American Civil War* (New York: Random House, 2008); Edward H. Bonekemper III, *The 10 Biggest Civil War Blunders* (Washington, DC: Regnery, 2018).

2. Abraham Lincoln, "By the President of the United States, A Proclamation," October 3, 1863, Obama White House Archives, accessed April 11, 2019, http://obamawhitehouse.archives.gov/sites/default/files/docs/transcript_for_abraham_lincoln_thanksgiving_proclamation_1863.pdf. See also "Lincoln and Thanksgiving," National Park Service, US Department of the Interior, accessed January 15, 2020, http://www.nps.gov/liho/learn/historyculture/lincoln-and-thanksgiving.htm.

3. Lincoln, "By the President of the United States, A Proclamation." See also "Lincoln and Thanksgiving."

4. Lincoln, "By the President of the United States, A Proclamation." See also "Lincoln and Thanksgiving."

5. Adapted from Robert Jeffress, "Count Blessings, Not Sheep," sermon, May 27, 2012, First Baptist Church of Dallas, Texas.

28. For Forgiving Others

1. All quotations and details about Frederick Douglass's life and American slavery come from: Frederick Douglass, *Life and Times of Frederick Douglass, Written by Himself. His Early Life as a Slave, His Escape from Bondage, And His Complete History to the Present Time* (Hartford, CT: Park, 1881); Frederick Douglass, *Narrative of the Life of Frederick Douglass, an American Slave*, 6th ed. (London: H. G. Collins, 1851).

29. For Wisdom

1. Facts for this chapter were found in the following sources: John Salmon, "'A Mission of the Most Secret and Important Kind': James Lafayette and American Espionage in 1781," *Virginia Cavalcade* 31 (1981): 78–85; Kenneth A. Daigler, *Spies, Patriots, and Traitors: American Intelligence in the Revolutionary War* (Washington, DC: Georgetown University Press, 2014), 226–227; Marquis de LaFayette, "To George Washington from Marie-Joseph-Paul-Yves-Roch-Gilbert Du Motier, Marquis De LaFayette, 25 August 1781," National Archives, August 25, 1781, accessed July 3, 2019, http://founders.archives.gov/documents/Washington/99-01-02-06792; "Petition for James, Slave Belonging to William Armistead, 30 November 1786," photo of legislative petition to the Virginia General Assembly, Box 179, Folder 10, (Richmond, Virginia: Library of Virginia), http://edu.lva.virginia.gov/online_classroom/lesson_plans/manumission_petition_for_james_lafayette; George Allan Cook, *John Wise: Early American Democrat* (Whitefish, MT: Literary Licensing LLC, 2012); J. M. Mackaye, "The Founder of American Democracy," *New England Magazine*, new series, 29 (September 1903–February 1904): 73–83, http://archive.org/stream/newenglandmagazi29bost#page/73/mode/1up; Eric D. Lehman, *Homegrown Terror: Benedict Arnold and the Burning of New London* (Middletown, CT: Wesleyan University Press, 2014). For the historical value of money today, I referenced the CPI Inflation Calculator, "U.S. Inflation Rate, $100 in 1790 to 2018," accessed January 15, 2020, http://www.officialdata.org/1790-dollars-in-2018.

30. For Discernment

1. Jonathan Edwards, *A Narrative of Surprising Conversions*, 1737 (repr., London: Counted Faithful, 2018); Jonathan Edwards, *Distinguishing Marks of a Work of the Spirit of God* (Kindle edition, n.d.).

2. Many facts for this chapter were found in the following sources: Melissa Petruzzello, "Second Great Awakening," *Encyclopaedia Britannica*, May 8, 2019, http://www .britannica.com/topic/Second-Great-Awakening; Charles G. Finney, *The Autobiography of Charles G. Finney*, ed. Helen Wessel (Bloomington, MN: Bethany House, 1977).

3. Susan J. White, *Christian Worship and Technological Change* (Nashville: Abingdon Press, 1994), 96.

4. Charles G. Finney, *Finney's Systematic Theology*, expanded edition (Bloomington, MN: Bethany House, 1994), 57, 179, 206, 209, 217, 320–322, 326–327; Charles G. Finney, *The Memoirs of Charles Finney: The Complete Restored Text* (Grand Rapids, MI: Academie, 1989), 53–54.

5. Charles G. Finney, *Sinners Bound to Change Their Own Hearts* (Orlando: GodSounds, 2016), 21–22; Charles G. Finney, *Finney's Systematic Theology*, expanded edition (Bloomington, MN: Bethany House, 1994), 224, 236.

6. Marsha West, "The Charles Finney Cornucopia of False Doctrine, Pelagianism & Evangelical Manipulation," Christian Research Network, January 15, 2019, http:// christianresearchnetwork.org/2019/01/15/the-charles-finney-cornucopia-of-false -doctrine-pelagianism-evangelical-manipulation; and Jared Moore, "'Charles Finney: The Great Distorter of Christian Truth in Our Age'—Michael Horton," SBC Voices, March 11, 2013, https://sbcvoices.com/charles-finney-the-greatest-distorter-of -christian-truth-in-our-age-michael-horton.

7. B. B. Warfield, *Studies in Perfectionism*, 2 vols. (New York: Oxford, 1932), 2:23–24.

8. Iain H. Murray, *Revival and Revivalism* (Carlisle, PA: Banner of Truth, 1994).

31. For Personal Repentance

1. Charles Colson, "Chuck Colson —How God Turned Around Nixon's Hatchet Man," speech given at the Veritas Forum at Columbia University, 2008, posted April 23, 2012, 13:40–13:44, http://www.youtube.com/watch?v=r_OqvFJhDRY.

2. Some facts for this chapter were found in the following sources: Charles W. Colson, *Born Again, with New Introduction and Epilogue* (Grand Rapids, MI: Chosen Books, 2008); Bob Woodward and Carl Bernstein, *All the President's Men* (New York: Simon & Schuster, 1974); "Watergate Scandal," History.com, updated September 25, 2019, http://www.history.com/topics/1970s/Watergate; "The Legacy of Chuck Colson," Prison Fellowship, accessed June 10, 2019, http://www.prisonfellowship.org/about /chuckcolson; Colson, "Chuck Colson—How God Turned Around"; Charles Colson, interview with the *700 Club* on the Christian Broadcasting Network, "Chuck Colson: 35 Years of Faith—CBN.com," 2008, accessed June 10, 2019, http://www .chuckcolsonstory.com.

32. For Those Deceived by False Religions

1. Many of these teachings are found in the Qur'an and other Muslim sacred writings. Note: Many English translations of the Qur'an are poor or misleading in nature, often reflecting sectarian and political biases of the translators. However, two good English

translations of the Qur'an are A. J. Arberry, *The Koran Interpreted, a Translation* (London: Allen & Unwin), 1955, and Usama Dakdok, *The Generous Qur'an* (Venice, FL: Usama Dakdok Publishing, 2009). Other facts for this chapter were found in the following sources: Nabeel Qureshi, *No God but One: Allah or Jesus? A Former Muslim Investigates the Evidence for Islam and Christianity* (Grand Rapids, MI: Zondervan, 2016); Muhammad Ibn Ismaiel Al-Bukhari, *The Translation of the Meanings of Sahih Al-Bukhari: Arabic-English (English and Arabic Edition)*, 1st ed., trans. Muhammad M. Khan (Houston: Dar-us-Salam Publications, 1997), http://thechoice.one/sahih-al-bukhari -hadith-in-english-all-volumes-1-9; David Wood, "Muhammad's Child Bride (Tract)," Acts 17 Apologetics, November 30, 2018, http://acts17.org/2018/11/30/muhammads -child-bride-tract; Martin Lings, *Muhammad: His Life Based on the Earliest Sources* (Rochester, VT: Inner Traditions International, 1983); Josh Hanrahan, "'Islam Brought Me Nothing but Pain and Hardship': Iranian Child Bride Who Was Beaten by Her Husband and Then Forced to Give Up Her Children to Flee to Australia Slams Harsh Muslim Regime," *Daily Mail*, updated December 3, 2017, http://www.dailymail.co.uk /news/article-5140283/Muslim-woman-tells-story-child-bride-Iran.html; Robert Morey, *The Islamic Invasion* (Eugene, OR: Harvest House Publishers, 1992), 177–208; David Wood, "Muhammad: The White Prophet with Black Slaves," Answering Muslims, Acts 17 Apologetics, February 12, 2016, accessed April 23, 2019, http://www .answeringmuslims.com/2016/02/muhammad-white-prophet-with-black-slaves.html; Joseph Smith, *Teachings of the Prophet Joseph Smith*, ed. Joseph Fielding Smith (Salt Lake City: Deseret Book Company, 1938); Joseph Smith et al., *Doctrine and Covenants*, 2013 edition (Salt Lake City: Church of Jesus Christ of Latter-Day Saints, 2013); Bruce R. McConkie, *Mormon Doctrine* (Salt Lake City: Deseret Book Company, 1966); Joseph Smith, *Pearl of Great Price*, ed. Franklin D. Richards (Salt Lake City: Deseret News Company, 1851); "Mormon Church Admits for First Time That Founder Joseph Smith Had a 14-Year-Old Bride," HuffPost, updated December 6, 2017, https://www .huffpost.com/entry/mormon-joseph-smith-teen-bride_n_6054272; Lindsay Hansen Park, "Utah's Underage Marriage Problem," *Utah Bee*, November 20, 2018, http://www .theutahbee.com/2018/11/20/utahs-underage-marriage-problem; "Mormons and Paiutes Murder 120 Emigrants at Mountain Meadows," History.com, last updated September 9, 2019, http://www.history.com/this-day-in-history/mormons-and-paiutes-murder-120 -emigrants-at-mountain-meadows; Edward Dalcour, "Mormonism and Black Skin," Department of Christian Defense, February 8, 2018, http://christiandefense.org/ mormonism/mormonism-and-black-skin.

33. For Bible Literacy

1. As far as we can tell, every single Founding Father wanted general Christian principles promoted in the public square. Mark David Hall, "Did America Have a Christian Founding?," Heritage Foundation, June 7, 2011, http://www.heritage.org/political -process/report/did-america-have-christian-founding.
2. Hall, "Did America Have a Christian Founding?."
3. Thomas Jefferson, "Proclamation Appointing a Day of Thanksgiving and Prayer, 11 November 1779," National Archives, http://founders.archives.gov/documents /Jefferson/01-03-02-0187.
4. Benjamin Franklin, during debates in the Constitutional Convention, June 28, 1787, Philadelphia, "Madison Debates," archived by the Avalon Project, Lillian Goldman Law

Library, Yale Law School, accessed May 31, 2019, http://avalon.law.yale.edu
/18th_century/debates_628.asp.

5. Adapted from Robert Jeffress, "America Is a Christian Nation," sermon, June 24, 2018, First Baptist Church of Dallas, Texas.

6. John Fea, interview with Jonathan Petersen, "History of the American Bible Society: An Interview with John Fea," Bible Gateway, May 23, 2016, http://www.biblegateway .com/blog/2016/05/history-of-the-american-bible-society-an-interview-with-john-fea.

7. John Jay, as quoted by Joseph Loconte, "Why Religious Values Support American Values," Heritage Foundation, September 26, 2005, http://www.heritage.org/civil -society/report/why-religious-values-support-american-values. Other facts for this chapter were found in Mark David Hall, "Christianity and the American Founding," Azusa Pacific University Koch Lecture, July 11, 2012, http://www.youtube.com /watch?v=_978ZVPqw4w.

8. Kenneth Berding, "The Crisis of Biblical Illiteracy and What We Can Do about It," *Biola Magazine*, June 2014, http://magazine.biola.edu/article/14-spring/the-crisis-of -biblical-illiteracy; Barna Group, "The State of the Bible, 2014," report commissioned by the American Bible Society, 2014, http://www.americanbible.org/uploads/content /state-of-the-bible-data-analysis-american-bible-society-2014.pdf.

9. Bob Smietana, "LifeWay Research: Americans Are Fond of the Bible, Don't Actually Read It," LifeWay Research, April 25, 2017, http://lifewayresearch.com/2017/04/25 /lifeway-research-americans-are-fond-of-the-bible-dont-actually-read-it.

10. R. Albert Mohler Jr., "The Scandal of Biblical Illiteracy: It's Our Problem," AlbertMohler.com, January 20, 2016, http://albertmohler.com/2016/01/20/the -scandal-of-biblical-illiteracy-its-our-problem-4.

34. For Courageous Pastors

1. Vikram Johri, "'Alexis de Tocqueville': The First French Critic of the US," *Christian Science Monitor*, April 10, 2007, http://www.csmonitor.com/2007/0410/p15s01 -bogn.html.

2. Henry Jones Ford, *The Scotch-Irish in America* (Princeton, NJ: Princeton University Press, 1915), 583–587.

3. Ambrose Serle to Lord Dartmouth, November 8, 1776, in *B. F. Stevens' Facsimiles of Manuscripts in European Archives Relating to America 1773-1783, with Descriptions, Editorial Notes, Collations, References and Translations*, vol. 24, ed. Benjamin F. Stevens (repr., Wilmington, DE: Mellifont Press, 1970), 2045.

4. Carl Bridenbaugh, *Mitre and Sceptre: Transatlantic Faiths, Ideas, Personalities, and Politics, 1689–1775* (New York: Oxford University Press, 1962), xi; Kevin Phillips, *The Cousins' Wars: Religion, Politics, and the Triumph of Anglo-America* (New York: Basic Books, 1999), xxi–xxii, 16, 92, 177; Edmund Burke, *The Works of the Right Honourable Edmund Burke. Vol. VI with an Introduction by F. W. Raffety* (New York: Oxford University Press, 1907), 244, 358, http://archive.org/details/in.ernet.dli.2015.97422 /page/n11; James Graham Leyburn, *The Scotch-Irish: A Social History* (Chapel Hill: University of North Carolina Press, 1962), 305.

5. Alexis de Tocqueville, "Of the Manner in Which Religion in the United States Avails Itself of Democratic Tendencies," chap. 5 in *Democracy in America, Volume II*, trans. Henry Reeve (London: Saunders and Otley, 1840).

6. From Robert Jeffress, "For Pastors Only (America's Last Hope)," sermon, October 30, 2011, First Baptist Church of Dallas, Texas.

35. For Churches

1. Many facts for this chapter were found in the following sources: Michael Ray, "Battle of Midway," *Encyclopaedia Britannica*, last updated November 6, 2019, http://www .britannica.com/event/Battle-of-Midway; "Battle of Midway," History.com, last updated December 17, 2019, http://www.history.com/topics/world-war-ii/battle-of -midway; Cornelius Ryan, *The Longest Day* (New York: Simon & Schuster, 1959); Dave Roos, "D-Day: Facts on the Epic 1944 Invasion That Changed the Course of WWII," History.com, updated June 5, 2019, http://www.history.com/topics/world- war-ii/d-day; Franklin D. Roosevelt, "A 'Mighty Endeavor:' D-Day," radio address to the nation, June 6, 1944, Franklin D. Roosevelt Presidential Library and Museum, National Archives, accessed January 16, 2020, http://www.fdrlibrary.org/d-day; "V-J Day," History.com, updated March 14, 2019, http://www.history.com/topics/world -war-ii/v-j-day. Parts of this chapter were also taken from Robert Jeffress, "Straight Answers to Tough Questions," sermon, September 12, 2010, First Baptist Church of Dallas, Texas.

36. For Victory in Spiritual Warfare

1. Portions of this chapter are derived from Robert Jeffress, "Blueprint for Your Destruction," chap. 3 in *The Divine Defense* (Colorado Springs: WaterBrook, 2006).
2. Liza Porteus, "U.S. Bags 'Baghdad Bob,'" Fox News, last updated January 13, 2015, http://www.foxnews.com/story/2003/06/25/report-us-bags-baghdad-bob.html.
3. Rakesh Kochnar, "How Americans Compare with the Global Middle Class," Pew Research Center, July 9, 2015, http://www.pewresearch.org/fact-tank/2015/07/09 /how-americans-compare-with-the-global-middle-class.

37. For Steadfastness in Persecution

1. Linley Sanders, "Who Is Jack Phillips? Meet the Christian Baker in the Masterpiece Cakeshop Supreme Court Case," *Newsweek*, December 5, 2017, http://www .newsweek.com/who-jack-phillips-meet-christian-baker-735094; Jack Phillips, "Jack Phillips: Despite My Court Win, Colorado Civil Rights Commission Is Coming after Me Again," *USA Today*, updated August 16, 2018, http://www.usatoday.com/story /opinion/2018/08/16/jack-phillips-despite-my-supreme-court-victory-im-still-under -attack-column/996588002.
2. Leonardo Blair, "Minutes after Sunday School Class Said They Would Die for Christ, Half Killed in Sri Lankan Bomb Blast," *Christian Post*, April 22, 2019, http://www .christianpost.com/news/minutes-after-sunday-school-class-said-they-would-die-for -christ-half-killed-in-sri-lankan-bomb-blast.html.
3. Quintus Septimus Florense Tertullianus, *Apologeticus* (Roman Empire, late second century), chapter 50; Joyce Ellen Salisbury, *The Blood of Martyrs: Unintended Consequences of Ancient Violence* (New York: Routledge, 2004); David Wright and Philip F. Esler, "Tertullian," in *The Early Christian World*, vol. 2 (London: Routledge, 2000), 1027–1047. See also Acts 8:4 for an early example of persecution leading to the spread of the gospel.
4. Based on data from "2019 World Watch List reporting period, November 1, 2017– October 31, 2018," Open Doors USA, accessed April 23, 2019, http://www .opendoorsusa.org/christian-persecution.
5. Adapted from Robert Jeffress, "When Persecution Comes," sermon, November 6, 2011, First Baptist Church of Dallas, Texas.

6. Derived from Joseph Sneed, "A Prayer for Persecuted Christians," prayer card (Dallas: Pathway to Victory, August 2017).

38. Against Spiritual Blindness

1. "Fanny Crosby: Prolific and Blind Hymn Writer," in *131 Christians Everyone Should Know* (Nashville: Holman Reference, 2000).
2. "Fanny Crosby: Prolific and Blind Hymn Writer."
3. Some facts for this chapter were found in the following sources: Fanny J. Crosby, *Fanny J. Crosby: An Autobiography* (Peabody, MA: Hendrickson Publishers, 2008); "Fanny Crosby: Prolific and Blind Hymn Writer"; "Fanny Crosby," *Encyclopaedia Britannica*, March 20, 2019, https://www.britannica.com/biography/Fanny-Crosby; "Fanny Crosby: America's Hymn Queen," Christianity.com, April 28, 2010, http://www .christianity.com/church/church-history/timeline/1801-1900/fanny-crosby-americas -hymn-queen-11630385.html.

39. For Revival

1. Information for this chapter came from: Patrick Morley, "A Brief History of Spiritual Revival and Awakening in America," ChurchLeaders.com, June 4, 2019, http:// churchleaders.com/outreach-missions/outreach-missions-articles/257668-brief-history -spiritual-revival-awakening-america.html; Earle E. Cairns, *An Endless Line of Splendor: Revivals and Their Leaders from the Great Awakening to the Present* (Eugene, OR: Wipf and Stock Publishers, 2015); Elgin Sylvester Moyer, *Great Leaders of the Christian Church* (Chicago: Moody Press, 1951), 457; J. Edwin Orr, *The Second Evangelical Awakening*, abridged version (London: Marshall, Morgan and Scott, 1955); Eddie L. Hyatt, *The Great Prayer Awakening of 1857–58: The Prayer Movement That Ended Slavery and Saved the American Union* (Grapevine, TX: Hyatt Press, 2019).

40. For Evangelism

1. Facts for this chapter were found in the following sources: Jackson Spielvogel, *Western Civilization: A Brief History*, 10th ed. (Boston: Cengage, 2019); Philip Hughes, *A History of the Church to the Eve of the Reformation: Beginnings to Byzantine Catholicism* (Edmond, OK: Veritatis Splendor Publications, 2012); "Gutenberg Bible," *Encyclopaedia Britannica*, last updated January 27, 2016, http://www.britannica .com/topic/Gutenberg-Bible; "Morse Code and the Telegraph," History.com, updated June 6, 2019, http://www.history.com/topics/inventions/telegraph; "Reginald Aubrey Fessenden," *Encyclopaedia Britannica*, updated October 28, 2011, http:// www.britannica.com/biography/Reginald-Aubrey-Fessenden; "The Roaring Twenties History," History.com, updated May 16, 2019, http://www.history.com/topics/roaring -twenties/roaring-twenties-history; Richard Greene, "'Puff Graham,'" *Decision Magazine*, April 1, 2018, http://decisionmagazine.com/puff-graham; "Profile: William (Billy) F. Graham, Jr.," Billy Graham Evangelistic Association, updated January 1, 2020, http://billygraham.org/about/biographies/billy-graham; Kat Eschner, "The Farmboy Who Invented Television," *Smithsonian Magazine*, August 28, 2017, http:// www.smithsonianmag.com/smart-news/farmboy-who-invented-television-while -plowing-180964607; Evan Andrews, "Who Invented the Internet?," History.com, updated October 28, 2019, http://www.history.com/news/who-invented-the-internet.

About the Author

★ ★ ★

DR. ROBERT JEFFRESS is Senior Pastor of the 14,000-member First Baptist Church in Dallas, Texas, and a Fox News contributor. He is also an adjunct professor at Dallas Theological Seminary. Dr. Jeffress has made more than two thousand guest appearances on various radio and television programs and regularly appears on major mainstream media outlets such as Fox News channel's *Fox and Friends*, *The O'Reilly Factor*, *Hannity*, *Lou Dobbs Tonight*, *Varney and Co.*, and *Judge Jeanine*; ABC's *Good Morning America*; and HBO's *Real Time with Bill Maher*. Dr. Jeffress hosts a daily radio program, *Pathway to Victory*, that is heard nationwide on more than eight hundred stations in major markets such as Dallas–Fort Worth, New York City, Chicago, Los Angeles, Washington, DC, Houston, and Seattle. His weekly television program can be seen in 195 countries and on 11,283 cable and satellite systems throughout the world, including China, and on the Trinity Broadcasting Network and Daystar.

Dr. Jeffress is the author of more than twenty books, including *Choosing the Extraordinary Life*, *When Forgiveness Doesn't Make Sense*, *Countdown to the Apocalypse*, and *Not All Roads Lead to Heaven*. Dr. Jeffress recently led his congregation in the completion of a $135 million re-creation of its downtown campus. The project is the largest in modern church history and serves as a "spiritual oasis" covering 6 blocks of downtown Dallas.

Dr. Jeffress has a DMin from Southwestern Baptist Theological Seminary, a ThM from Dallas Theological Seminary, and a BS from Baylor University. In May 2010 he was awarded a Doctor of Divinity degree from Dallas Baptist University, and in June 2011 he received the Distinguished Alumnus of the Year award from Southwestern Baptist Theological Seminary.

Dr. Jeffress and his wife, Amy, have two daughters, Julia and Dorothy, and a son-in-law, Ryan Sadler.